WINTER OF THE GENOMES

Larry Kilham

Published by
FutureBooks.info
Available for purchase from:
CreateSpace.com
Amazon.com
and other retailers

ISBN: 1500822051
ISBN 13: 9781500822057
Library of Congress Control Number: 2014914549
CreateSpace Independent Publishing Platform
North Charleston, South Carolina

To my mother, who long ago
wanted me to write this book,
and who never had the chance to read it.

CONTENTS

Part 3
Robots as Part of the Ecosystem

Part 4
The Road Ahead

FORWARD

Larry Kilham's fast-moving, concise and compelling book is both a real-time history of robotic development and a sober, realistic consideration of the role robots might play in ameliorating—or aggravating—the serious problems that our world faces as it careens headlong into the twenty-first century. It's clear that both outcomes are possible, often simultaneously. How to maximize the first and minimize the second is the question.

I call it a "real time" history because events are unfolding almost faster than we can write about them, and certainly faster than we can understand and assess their impacts. This is happening because the excitement of the field and its economic impact have attracted many of the world's brightest humans— from the worlds of science and technology but also from finance and government. Sometime in the future it may also attract the best robotic minds as well. We shall see.

We don't know yet whether robots will ever be truly creative or thoughtful or emotional, but it is already quite clear that they can far outperform people in any activity that smacks of mere repetition or speed or strength. It is programmed computation and microelectronics that make this possible. What robots can already do—at low cost, with low environmental impact and with none of the neediness of human beings— makes makes their attractive side almost irresistible. As is often the case with human endeavors, the downsides are left for later generations to solve.

Nobody knows how many people the Earth can support, but we are in the midst of a gigantic experiment that is likely to tell us the answer. With our population at more than seven billion, having doubled over the last 25 years, our physical world and all of its inhabitants are being stressed to the point of imminent collapse. While there have been several cataclysmic epochs in Earth's history, there has never before been one caused by human beings. There is simply no doubt that this one is. Appropriately enough, our era is called "the Anthropocene."

Clearly, rapid growth in population is driving this problem. Already it has become obvious that there simply isn't enough water or raw materials on Earth to allow us to continue on our present rapacious trajectory. It's also clear that our lack of expansionary restraint has led to devastating impacts to our precious biosphere—the the home for life as we know it on Earth. Whether one speaks of global climate change, or the poisoning of the oceans or the huge diminishment of natural species, mankind owns these problems. They will only be solved by people and nations working together to find much wiser ways of stewardship. Free markets will play an essential role, but so also will extensive national and international planning.

Our hope must be that if mankind created these problems it should be smart enough to solve them. Doing so will require great creativity and good will, not to mention a sense of urgency. Unfortunately, the issues are likely to become all the more complex because of unintended consequences. No one knows how societies will respond should massive unemployment arise due to the emergence of large robotic populations. Perhaps even more importantly, no one knows how people will respond to the lack of meaningful work in their lives.

Of course no one yet knows how this complex tale going to turn out. Larry Kilham's book is an important contribution to how we should be thinking about the existential task before us.

Robert Eisenstein
Founding Director, Santa Fe Alliance for Science
Former President, Santa Fe Institute

INTRODUCTION

The wind blew gently through the whispering white pines towering above. The pasture grass smelled sweet, and there were the rasps of the locusts and the calls of the meadowlarks. The bees were darting in and out of the apple blossoms. I was dozing in the warm sun against my horse, Gramps, who was also dozing, and snuggled against both of us was my dog, Axel. I was a contented part of the natural universe and so were all the creatures there.

That was six decades ago. Today, if I were a young man, I would wake up and reach for my smartphone. My world would be my friends and information offerings competing for my attention. Nature would be an afterthought and, at best, a limitless source of food and natural resources. My snuggly friend could be a cute robot who placed minimal demands on anything or anybody. The meadowlarks long since have disappeared. And the bees? That's a question we will explore later.

Under pressure from critically declining resources, population increases, and the cerebral grip of the information technologies, we have lost our way. We are starting to embrace robots to coddle us and do ever more of our work. The robots are but one manifestation of artificial intelligence (AI). AI can make life more productive and is said to give us relationships we trust more than with humans.

•••

Ever since the Industrial Revolution, we have blissfully trampled upon the environment and gobbled up natural resources in an attitude of hubris of the species. Man has always prided himself on his intelligence, which raises him above all other living things in taking advantage of his resources. His intelligence is unique in that man has the capacity to be thoughtful and creative. No other species can make that claim. Unfortunately, the creativity has often been used for selfish purposes.

Yet there are many species with much smaller brains—honey bees for example—who in some ways seem just as intelligent as us or more so. These tiny creatures pass their lifetime finding succulent flowers and managing a hive. The bees learn and remember, and they carry out such apparently human functions as group decision-making and job specialization. Their consciousness does not extend, however, beyond their immediate world; they have little or no self-awareness; and they are not capable of abstract thinking.

Where there is a high degree of hive-like specialization and repetition in the human world, such as in automobile assembly plants, smartphone production, or insurance companies, there is less need to be creative than in entrepreneurial ventures. AI and robots will increasingly be employed in those hives. I will uncover many other areas, some unexpected, where AI and robots will have a strong future.

It is also true that humans have been the only species to accumulate knowledge in reference collections called libraries and data clouds. The most intelligent birds and animals do this only to a very small degree except for specialized needs like migratory navigation or techniques of nest building. The designers of AI and robots will exploit the human-built data banks, however. They will build into their machines the required reference information and provide for automatic updating.

We should not think of AI as an intellectual competitor of humans. A limited number of special AI computers in a few decades may have significantly more intelligence than humans do, but those computers are not likely to have a high degree of self-awareness or the capability of unfettered abstract thinking. The use of AI and robots will be no different from the use of seeing-eye dogs, homing pigeons, robotic vacuum cleaners, or factory assembly robots—they all have less intelligence than humans do, but they are used because they are more efficient than humans in their area of specialty. To make sense of all of this, we must view humans, nature, and all forms of AI as one ecosystem. Each species can alter the futures of the other species.

Increasing automation is likely to reduce the number of jobs. This dimming employment outlook, family planning, and women's new sense of independence, are leading couples and single women to conclude that that they should have fewer or no children. This has been the case already in such advanced and populous countries as Japan, Italy and Germany. Their populations are shrinking. Even India, often mentioned as a paradigm of uncontrolled population, has seen its birth rate decline to the no-growth level. The smaller populations could significantly reduce energy consumption, thereby reducing global warming to a tolerable level.

If this trend continues and expands over several generations and many countries, the earth's population could shrink after several generations to well below today's seven billion. The world's economic, social and natural life systems will be searching for new forms and a new equilibrium.

PART 1

THE NEW SPECIES: AI AND ROBOTS

MAN AND MACHINES

For centuries, it seemed that man had reached equilibrium with the natural world around him. True, some species, like passenger pigeons, were wiped out, but on the whole, everything seemed satisfactory. The effects of pollution and resource depletion seemed manageable, could be postponed, or could be cured by new technology.

Then a new group of beings arose: AI and robots. These started out as simple as thermostats. Then one emerged as a super AI computer that beat chess masters. They became acceptable options in commerce and industry.

As I talk to people in all walks of life about AI and robots, most of the time I find emotional resistance to having a straightforward discussion. I might ask, "What do you think about the prospects of robots doing many of our daily jobs?"

"That's going to happen, but I'm afraid that the machines are going to take over," some answer.

"But the scientists say that robots don't pass any major intelligence test—they will never be smarter than us," I add reassuringly, but it falls on deaf ears.

The first popular response to this frightening possibility was by the pioneering science fiction author, Isaac Asimov. He postulated the Three Laws of Robotics:

1 – A robot may not injure a human being or, through inaction, allow a human being to come to harm.

2 – A robot must obey orders given to it by human beings, except where such orders would conflict with the First Law.

3 – A robot must protect its own existence as long as such protection does not conflict with the First or Second Law.

The emotional level was ratcheted up considerably when inventor and futurist, Ray Kurzweil, proposed the Singularity point in his book, *The Singularity is Near.* "The Singularity will represent the culmination of the merger of our biological thinking and existence with our technology, resulting in a world that is human but transcends our biological roots." In an interview about that book, Kurzweil said: "We'll get to a point where technical progress will be so fast that unenhanced human intelligence will be unable to follow it. That will mark the Singularity." This has often been interpreted in simplest terms to be when computers exceed humans in intelligence.

The whole issue of computer intelligence is unsettling for many—maybe most—people. The reason is that we cannot seem to deal with an issue that would appear to put us in second place in position, strength or intellect to anything, let alone computers.

•••

Our perception of ourselves with respect to the rest of the observable landscape and universe has been bandied about since at least the Renaissance. While it is easy to say, "Our home, the earth, is just another planet in just another solar system in just another galaxy," it would not have been easy to say that 500 years ago. With no celestial database, why should we not have assumed that the earth is the center of the universe? After all, the earth is where people are, and people are superior to everything else.

Nicolaus Copernicus (1473-1543), a Polish mathematician and astronomer, broke new ground when he formulated a heliocentric model of "the universe" with the sun at the center and the earth as just one of the planets orbiting around it. Other scientists of the time also developed heliocentric models of the universe, the best-known being Galileo Galilei (1564-1642), an Italian. The scientific revolution was underway.

As the world turned its scientific lens inward, Charles Darwin (1809-1882), an English naturalist and geologist, focused the world's attention on evolution and species. He summarized his evolutionary theory in the introduction to his *On the Origin of species*:

> As many more individuals of each species are born than can possibly survive; and as, consequently, there is a frequent recurring struggle for existence, it follows that any being, if it vary however slightly in any manner profitable to itself, under the complex and sometimes varying conditions of life, will have a better chance of surviving, and thus be *naturally selected*. From the strong principle of inheritance, any selected variety will tend to propagate its new and modified form.

We—plants, animals, humans and microorganisms—all are in a race for survival through species improvement. Darwin, moreover, implied that human beings evolved from animals, to the horror of his readers. Humans are just somewhat more intelligent and clever than any other species. He delved further into that intriguing species, humans, in his books *The Descent of Man in Relation to Sex* and *The Expression of Emotion in Man and Animals*. These revelations, coming from one of the most respected scientists of the time, were very difficult for the proper Victorians to accept.

As the Victorians were absorbing the chastening insights of Darwin, however, their engineers and industrialists were among the leaders of the Industrial Revolution. It reaffirmed, at least for the common person, the near god-like status of man. Who could not be thrilled by the puffing and hissing of powerful steam engines with their beautiful mechanisms rotating and clanking in plain view? The feeling might have been akin to a youngster today watching a rocket blast off for space.

Six million people visited the 1851 World's Fair in London. In a huge, specially designed building called the Crystal Palace, opened by Queen Victoria and Prince Albert, exhibitors from thirty-two countries showed the hitherto unimaginable progress brought by new machines and the industrial system. Meanwhile, huge factories in the industrial West and later the rest of the world, were churning out machine-produced products ranging from kitchenware to textiles. Later, they took on the challenge of the mass-production of automobiles and airplanes.

It was the best of times and the worst of times. Wealthy aristocracies and empires based on manufacturing and trading of resources emerged to dominate much of the world. Their miraculous factories were employing millions in miserable Dickensian conditions and, while not always obvious at the time, pollution and depletion of resources began. Only a very small minority of the industrial and urban populations enjoyed being the humans who were be the Center of All Things. Man was improving his position among all the species but at a price.

In 1953, there was another humbling challenge to anthropocentricity, the perception of everything according to human values, when James Watson (American, 1928-) and Francis Crick (English, 1916-2004) discovered DNA at Cambridge University in England. Maurice Wilkins and Rosalind Franklin also made major contributions. They found that twisted pairs of DNA strands could be pulled apart, like cheap plastic zippers, and their genetic code could then be passed to newly forming organisms. Some leading scientists have concluded that the sole purpose in life of humans (or any other living organisms) is to pass genetic traits on to the next generation.

DNA molecules for a given purpose, such as determining eye color, are combined to form a gene, and a complete package of genes defining an organism is called a genome. The genome is the complete collection of genes that defines an organism. It controls everything about the organism ranging from its size and shape to the construction details of each of its organs. The male genome and the female genome combine and a new genome of the offspring is formed. It incorporates features from both parents' genomes and some random changes as well. If the offspring is an improvement over the prior generations, with no important new weaknesses, it will be a contributor to the evolution of the species, as described by Darwin. There are over 20,000 genes in a human genome. The tiny fruit fly, surprisingly, has about half that many.

So now that man has been defined by a genome broadly similar to any other animal's genome, are we left to be disillusioned wanderers in a world threatened by severe overpopulation, exhaustion of critical resources, and climate and other environmental change? Not necessarily. The Information

Revolution has produced an invention that signals the beginning of a new way for man to perceive himself in the world and the universe. This is the smartphone and all the variations of it. In fact, Ray Kurzweil, in an interview with the *New York Times*, responding to a question about the pending Singularity, said, "It's not us versus them...AI today is not in three or four dark federal intelligence agencies; it's in billions of mobile devices around the world."

People have discovered a completely new way to interact with others. Through mobile devices and social media many people are increasingly finding more sense of support with friends and strangers on the Internet, and even robots, AI machines and Internet avatars, than with their own family and associates. Thus, Sherry Turkle, MIT Professor of the Social Studies of Science and Technology, has aptly called her book on the subject *Alone Together: Why We Expect More from Technology and Less from Each Other*.

People also increasingly look to aggregated databases in the computer clouds, which can be found through Google and other online searches, rather than in libraries or other data collections. I called this communal world of data resources the Knowosphere in my book, *MegaMinds: How to Create and Invent in the Age of Google*. It, all smartphones, and other computers create a vast network surrounding the world in cyberspace. Susan Greenfield, Oxford University Neuroscientist, says:

> If you're constantly in front of a computer screen, you're the passive recipient of lots of information. You're just a consumer, living at the moment, having an experience, pressing buttons and reacting, but not having a life narrative any more. You're not defined by your family, or by what you know, or by specific events in the real world,

because most of your time is spent in cyberspace. So what are you? Could it be that we are just nodes on a much larger collective thought machine?

The group, the crowd, the world has replaced the individual. If man were ever the center of all things, it no longer looks like the case. A person is just another address in an amorphous mass. In view of this paradigm shift, AI and robots continue their penetration into our lives. Imagination, creativity, and interpersonal communications, which have been the human advantages over all other creatures, could wither away. The environment has changed from what you can see around you but you do not explore to what you can find on the Internet and which you can constantly explore.

•••

Which brings us back to robots. They and AI have been taking over jobs, but so far, there has not been a Luddite reaction. Automobile assembly and airline reservations are examples of automation's strong inroads. Yet an Oxford University study calculates that robots may take 47% of US jobs by 2033. A lot of this job shrinkage is in what Santa Fe Institute Professor Brian Arthur calls the "second economy" in the form of digital automation.

On the brighter side, robots are also making inroads as personal companions. They are often packaged as cuddly animals, and are used as companions for the elderly and even as assistants in nursing homes. Robots do not abuse the patients and can be more consistently caring than human caregivers can. Japan, where many robots have been developed and are manufactured, is counting on robots to help solve their care of the aging challenge brought about by a growing population of the elderly and shrinking population of workers. Children in the preteen ages can develop attachments to personal robots more than to people or pets. Professor Turkle reports that children find robots as "alive enough." She asks, "If a robot makes you love it, is it alive?"

It seems safe to assume that, at least for now, AI and robotics are here to stay and that their penetration in the US and industrial world will increase rapidly for the foreseeable future. The world robot population almost doubled from 4.49 million to 8.37 million from 2006 to 2010, including industrial and service robots, according to a study by the International Federation of Robotics. A quarter or more of the U.S. population could eventually be unemployed. In the remainder of this book, I will show where this all could lead.

2

CRISIS OF THE BEES

A look at the history and future of honeybees in the United States and elsewhere can give us a vivid example of the relationship among species and the possibilities of robots. It is unfortunate indeed that this story presents itself now because we are facing the possibility of catastrophic loss of the bee population. Honeybees, which are of the greatest commercial interest, pollinate about a third of what we eat, including fruits, nuts and vegetables. Thirty-one percent of US bee colonies were lost in the winter of 2013 alone. Given its extraordinarily long history, the honeybee species should have developed resistance to practically every pathogen.

There are only seven species of honeybees out of 20,000 known species of bees. The origins of honeybees trace back to the Cretaceous period about 130 million years ago. Indo-European honeybees survived the world's continents shifts and temperature changes. *Apis mellifera*, the honeybee species most common in the US today, began in Europe 2-3 million years ago.

Europeans brought *Apis mellifera* to the New World in 1622, and, through trade, the honeybees arrived in California in the 1850s. There were, however, 4,000 species of native bees (not honeybees) already in North America, and they still pollinate most of the native plants including pumpkins, watermelons, blueberries and cranberries.

Bee colonies are complex. The central figure is the queen bee, a fertile female. There are up to a thousand fertile male drone bees with which she can mate. Once a drone fertilizes the queen bee, he dies. The rest of the colony is sterile female worker bees. They typically number several tens of thousands.

The young worker bees carry out the housekeeping in the hive, build the honeycomb, and guard the hive. When they are older, the workers become the bees we are most familiar with, darting from blossom to blossom. Despite all this activity, the worker bees live less than a month while the queen lives 3-7 years.

There is a special worker bee called the scout. She tells the forager bees where the flowers are through choreographed dances in the hive. Through the dance moves, the scouts convey the distance to the food and its angle to the sun. The worker bee can visit 10 flowers a minute and may visit more than 600 flowers in one excursion.

•••

For many years all was well and with steady improvements for the beekeepers' procedures and equipment, the number of honeybees kept increasing. There were bothersome parasites and diseases like *Nosema Ceranae*, mites, hive beetles, and American foul brood, but these seemed manageable. Then around 2006, what is now a disaster began. Called Colony Collapse Disorder (CCD), this scourge wiped out 10 million beehives, valued at $2 billion, through 2013. Experts estimate that up to half of the $30 billion worth of crops in the US pollinated by honeybees could be lost. For six years, scientists could not isolate a definite mechanism for CCD. There were many dead ends and incomplete explanations.

Then in 2013, scientists at the University of Maryland and the US Department of Agriculture published in the journal PLOS ONE their list of pesticides and fungicides contaminating the pollen collected by the honeybees. They found eight chemicals, which reduced the bees' resistance to infection by *Nosema ceranae,* a microscopic spore-forming parasite. Bees that consumed pollen contaminated with fungicides were three times as likely to be infected by the parasite. Until this revelation, bees had not been thought to be affected by the presence of the fungicides.

The major culprit seems to be a class of pesticides called neonicotinoids, although mixtures of pesticides can also do great harm. Europe has banned the use of neonicotinoids for several years, and in 2013, the US EPA prohibited their use where bees are foraging or plants are flowering. These restrictions will help all bees. Wild bees are very important for pollination for both commercial crops and general flowering plants. Some wild bees produce honey.

While these are positive steps, the Chinese are going one-step further. In the southwest part of the country, where bees have almost been wiped out, farmers are hand pollinating apple and pear trees with pots of pollen and brushes. This is not a cost-effective solution for higher labor cost countries with smaller populations and may not be for China either.

●●●

Then, as the future of the honeybees seems dire indeed, the cavalry of the robots rushes to the rescue of the flowering plants and trees. Although they are not yet deployed into the waiting blossoms, they already have a name: robobees.

The current leader in robobees technology is a team at Harvard University. In May 2013, their School of Engineering and Applied Sciences announced that an experimental prototype of the robobee made its first controlled flight. Half the size of a paperclip, weighing less than a tenth of a gram, it powered upward, hovered on its delicate flapping wings, and flew away.

Writing in the *Scientific American*, the team leaders said, "In 2009 the three of us began to seriously consider what it would take to create a robotic bee colony. We wondered if mechanical bees could replicate not just an individual's behavior but the unique behavior that emerges out of interactions among thousands of bees. We have now created the first RoboBees—flying bee-size robots—and are working on methods to make thousands of them cooperate like a real hive."

A major engineering breakthrough was finding a way to power the high speed flapping of the 3 cm wings. The solution was piezoelectric effect actuators. Electric fields applied to tiny ceramic strips cause them to flap the bee's wings at 120 times per second.

The next challenge for the Harvard team is to develop a suitable internal source of bee power. There are a number of approaches to consider including an internal energy source such as a battery or a renewable source such as a photovoltaic cell on an attached plane.

Also to be developed is a way to cause a number of robobees to swarm and accomplish a coordinated task. Thousands of bees in one field will be required to pollinate several acres of crops.

•••

This brings us to the question of brains for the bees. Judged by our own intellectual standards, the artificial honeybee would need a brain at least as large as a personal computer. After all, a worker bee—the bee we are modeling—would need to know how to do housekeeping in the hive, defend it against attackers, seek out sources of pollen, gather the pollen, return to the hive, and tell the other bees where the pollen source is. Along the way, it would have to recognize the hive bees from alien bees and identify other insects and threats.

Marc Bekoff has written that bees know how to travel most efficiently between sites; they can distinguish complex landscape scenes including types of flowers; they consider social conditions, times of day and various sensory inputs; and they show memory ranging from days to entire life spans.

Melissa Bateson at Newcastle University in the United Kingdom has shown that when honeybees are stressed, they become pessimists. This behavior correlates with altered levels of dopamine, serotonin, and octopamine, which are involved with depression. In plain language, bees have at least some emotion—an unexpected attribute for a tiny brain.

The University of Sheffield in the United Kingdom has begun a project to model the honeybee's brain so that a version of the model can be loaded into a robobee. The project is called Green Brain. They will use massively paralleled PCs, or supercomputer clusters, to simulate and model the bee brain. In order to develop a simple and doable model for robobees, the Sheffield researchers are concentrating on the bee brain's vision and smell reception.

In addition to providing bee brains for the Harvard RoboBees project, the University of Sheffield team hopes to develop brains for many species of robots, which could substitute for many critically endangered or extinct species. It does not seem that this class of robots with their limited brains will pose a threat of overcoming humanity.

•••

Although we cannot be certain about how the honeybee CCD will play out, we can be sure that it is at the very least a harbinger of catastrophes to come for any number of species including mankind. These catastrophes could combine to what Thomas Lovejoy writing in the *Scientific American* calls a "Tsunami of Extinction."

First, there are the apparently inevitable changes happening as a result of climate change and the huge loss of forests and coral reefs. The International Union for Conservation of Nature estimates that 13 percent of bird, 25 percent of mammals and 41 percent of amphibian species may become extinct. These species losses cannot be replaced by evolution in the foreseeable future.

All grand-scale technological fixes seem utopian or create new problems. These include the geoengineering proposal of creating a stratospheric layer of sulfate aerosols to effectively cover the earth with a thin cloud to halt global warming. The mechanism would be similar to the blocking of sunlight by the dispersed ash of mega volcanoes. Starting the process is relatively easy. Small amounts of easily synthesized chemicals would be required, and they could be injected into the stratosphere by conventional military aircraft. Then the problems begin, including the high probability of life-supporting monsoons greatly reduced in Asia and Africa, further erosion of the ozone layer, and increased already catastrophic ocean acidification from the addition of acid rain. The atmospheric chemistry could change in many ways.

Of course, an old-fashioned pandemic could set off the human CCD (Civilization Collapse Disaster). The Black Death of the middle ages killed as many as 75 million people. The "Spanish flu" of 1918-1919 killed 50 million people worldwide. A similar flu, "bird flu," active among flocks in several countries, while not yet transmissible between humans, could become a pandemic threat in just a few mutations. If a pandemic like the flu occurs, it may be possible to use specially built robots to help quell the pending disaster. Thousands of these robots could tirelessly prepare vaccine doses and administer them to large populations.

This approach will not work with current technology against AIDS, which is a very real pandemic right now. Infection rates are as high as 25% in some African countries. Since the beginning of the epidemic, over 30 million people have died from AIDS-related causes.

Whether we are discussing the welfare of flora, fauna, or human beings, we must realize that we are about to pass through what Harvard biologist E.O. Wilson calls "a bottleneck unique in history." When we come out the other side in 50 or 100 years we should still have a diverse ecosystem with which we can live compatibly. He advises that key elements of a successful passage will be halting population growth and devising a wiser use of resources.

Other experts advise that the world's population must be reduced drastically and that people use much less resources. Currently, the world population is over seven billion. Within the lifetime of our elders, the world population has tripled. What is the maximum population that the world can sustain? There is a wide range of estimates by population specialists, and one to four billion seems to be where many are headed. This assumes living at reasonably modern standards.

Of course, we will hope that after all this chaos, the honey-bee will still be with us. They could be delightful associates in the scaled-down post-bottleneck ecosystem.

3

WHAT IS ARTIFICIAL INTELLIGENCE?

As the world cruises towards seemingly intractable problems such as overpopulation, depleted resources, and global warming, we will increasingly need breakthroughs of the kind that have been produced by ingenuity and insight. Artificial intelligence (AI) has been proposed as a solution for many future needs. What is AI, anyway?

The Merriam-Webster dictionary offers the following definition: "An area of computer science that deals with giving machines the ability to seem like they have human intelligence." We are back to the human-centered universe. The Free Dictionary is more open-minded: "The ability of a computer or other machine to perform those activities that are normally thought to require intelligence." I think even the simplest intelligence, such as the robobee, fits this definition.

First, let us dispel the startling statements and popular movie themes telling us that artificial intelligence will greatly exceed human intelligence in just a few decades. There have been startling statements and popular movies telling us that artificial intelligence will greatly exceed human intelligence in just a few decades. There may be little doubt that this will be the case for applications mostly requiring massive and repetitive computing, but is not so certain for projects requiring significant imagination and creativity. In any case, it is highly unlikely that androids will be running around conquering the world.

AI Computers can access very large databases. They can be used in detailed multidimensional design. They can manage vast projects. There is talk of computer-like nanorobots that can circulate around in your body. There are even computer programs to invent new devices. However, as far as I am aware, no computer independently came up with the general theory of relativity.

Since the explosion of electronics beginning roughly during WW II, there has been ever increasing interest in thinking machines. AI started with conventional electronic circuits wired to achieve an intelligent task. These circuits were built on "if...then..." logic. For example, "if the temperature is below 72 degrees, then turn on the heating; otherwise, leave the furnace off." In other words, the traditional home thermostat is a simple AI device. Simple electronic control circuits are the key to many successful industrial machines and consumer appliances today.

Increasingly, tiny single purpose computers called microprocessors or embedded systems have replaced electronic logic circuits. These can introduce more intelligence into the control system. Now we take for granted the availability of home controls that not only control temperature, but also manage the security system, lock and unlock doors, water the lawn, and remind you to walk the dog. Current model automobiles all depend on microprocessors for their operation and maintenance.

The penetration of simple AI is pervasive. Just as there are many times more insects than mammals, there are many more simple artificial intelligence devices than there are complex thinking computers. Cars, airplanes, boats, and space vehicles utilize countless simple AI control devices. These devices have an IQ of less than an ant's, but the technology has been perfected to a high degree of confidence, reliability and low cost.

Major opportunities to be creative in developing simple AI inventions today are in the nanotechnology arena. This is where the mechanical parts and circuits have been reduced in size to almost molecular scale. Applications range from smart phone controls to nanorobots cast adrift in the body to do good things such as attacking germs and tumors.

South Korean scientists are developing a treatment for cancer that is more efficient than chemotherapy. Microscopic robots carry the drugs. They are carried in modified salmonella bacteria, which are drawn to cancer cells by chemical attraction. They attack only the tumors, and the patient does not have side effects like losing hair whose cells normally would also be attacked.

Complex AI

If artificial intelligence could solve more complex problems and do large-scale useful jobs, this would be a payoff for humanity. These challenges could range from diagnosing diseases to managing manufacturing plants. I call this complex AI because complex computers and sophisticated sensors are involved. There will be ever more immense amounts of data, primarily stored in the computer clouds, and there will be software that sharpens its intelligence through continual learning. This can all be part of the Knowosphere.

The wakeup call came when IBM's Deep Blue supercomputer defeated Grandmaster Gary Kasparov in chess in 1997. Deep Blue's per circuit processing speeds are many fold faster than Kasparov's neuron processing speeds. It could examine more than 200 million chess moves per second!

The public really became aware of big AI when IBM's ultra super AI computer, Watson, beat two former winners of the television quiz show *Jeopardy!* Watson received the first prize of $1 million. The system is built around massively parallel processors. It uses IBM's *DeepQA* technology to generate hypotheses, gather massive evidence, and continue analyzing the data until a solution can be proposed. The system can process 500 gigabytes, the equivalent of a million books, per second. This program generally does not compute exact answers; it searches for the highest probability answer or solution. Watson was not designed to be creative, assuming that was possible.

Watson used encyclopedias, dictionaries, news sources, literary works and much more as sources. Watson would have to respond to the quiz questions in a few seconds, which, at the time, was thought impossible to do, but the machine clearly succeeded. IBM's first commercial applications of Watson have been mainly in healthcare. With its natural language communications with users, hypothesis generation, and evidence-based learning, it is a natural for use by medical professionals.

Another IBM supercomputer, Blue Gene, is analyzing the brain's structure and operation. It is analyzing its own creator! In 2005, the project was initiated at the Brain Mind Institute of the Ecole Polytechnique Fédérale de Lausanne in Switzerland. The computer can do up to 22.8 *trillion* operations per second. Each of its microprocessor chips simulates a single neuron, which is the basic go-no go logic unit in the brain. Each human brain has billions of them, which makes it too big even for Blue

Gene to simulate, so Henry Markram, the project's director, decided to simulate a rat's brain.

Actual simulations were run in mid-2008. The computer simulation produced behavior like a real neuron. Various cells did what they were supposed to do and in the proper sequences. The microprocessors were hooking themselves together and evolving into a cognitive mechanism similar to the core part of the mind. The research team was very encouraged and felt that Blue Brain appeared to demonstrate that their neurological model of the neocortex was correct.

However, scaling the model up to human brain size, where trillions of synapses are involved, would require about 500 petabytes of data (equivalent to 200 times Google's current total system wide computing capacity) and megawatts of electrical supply. What this means, at least for the present, is that current simulations of the human brain have come to a capacity limitation even for a super computer.

IBM's current research is to design systems that can learn from and interact with people. As Guruduth S. Banavar, director of IBM's cognitive computing research, told the *New York Times*, "The result should be way better than either a human or a computer system can do alone."

Brainlike Computers

Another approach in artificial intelligence is to avoid the use of precisely programmed digital computers and instead make an electronic computer that emulates the neurons and synapses of the brain. The strength of connections between neurons represents the relative strength from associating ideas, places, words, and the like. These connections can be strengthened or weakened with experience. This form of computing, sometimes called associative inference or thinking in analogies, is inexact compared to digital computing in standard (von Neumann architecture) computers but it is often much faster, uses much less power, can analyze with very incomplete data, and works despite some damage and noise in its structure.

The principles have been known since the artificial neuron experiments with simple electronics after World War II. Brainlike computers, often called cognitive computers, have only been built recently, however. Stanford University, California Institute of Technology, IBM, and Qualcomm are among the leaders with cognitive computer projects. These computers and others of their kind probably will be the basis of the most general application AI, which will be equivalent to the overall intelligence of the large mammals and humans.

In August 2014, IBM announced their brain-inspired computer chip. Called "TrueNorth," this chip has a million neurons—about as many as in the honeybee discussed in chapter 2. It carries out 46 billion synaptic operations per second in its 256 million programmable synapses and can be powered by a hearing aid battery. 5.4 billion transistors fit into a space the size of a postage stamp.

An important application for TrueNorth is video pattern recognition. It should be able to recognize people and objects in a scene. It should also do better speech recognition than the present systems, and consequently should find an immediate home in smartphones.

IBM has a goal of supplying devices for a 100 trillion synapse supercomputer—about the synapse count in the human brain—and at that point we will be well on our way to making HAL in *2001: A Space Odyssey* or the female computer person in the movie *Her*. Its energy consumption would be considerably less than a digital computer of similar capability, but much more than the human brain (20-40 watts). The power consumption will be an area for further improvement of the technology.

Among the variety of applications proposed for the IBM TrueNorth chip recently are:

- Provide sensory inputs to guide a blind person like a seeing eye dog would.
- Automate the surveillance input in real time for military and commercial drones.
- Serve as the core of a laboratory instrument to help scientists simulate brain functions.

Inventing with AI

You might breathe a little easier and think, "At least nature has the upper hand by continuous improvement through evolution. AI is only improved through human intervention." It is not quite that simple.

While it is highly unlikely that AI creatures will rise up and become our masters, the basic mechanism has been demonstrated for AI machines to improve themselves. Currently, the design-by-AI process has been focused on inventing and designing simple products. The genie is out of the bottle, however. Using similar design techniques, AI systems and robots could be asked to improve their own designs. The robobee could evolve itself into the super robobee. I think Darwin would be fascinated.

Inventing by use of an AI program has succeeded in a number of cases where the product to be invented involves one discipline such as mechanics or electronics and does not involve too many component parts. This emergent field has taken on the terms "genetic algorithms" or "evolutionary algorithms" because the design approach is evolutionary, seeking optimal success as various mutations are introduced.

An algorithm is a set of instructions to carry out carry out a procedure or process. It is usually in the form of a computer program derived from a set of equations or logical statements.

While genetic or evolutionary algorithms are usually best suited for the design of simple devices where one discipline is involved such as an electronic circuit of a few components, or the shape design for scissors, they have been used for the design of dams, bridges, gyroscopes and wind turbines.

Designing robots is an application of this approach, and there are reports about self-improving robots. Some robots design themselves—especially their control circuitry and pro-gramming—based on their trial-and-error results.

For example, you could start with a collection of shafts, wheels, sensors, structural kit parts and so forth and build a robot as a starting genotype as described for circuit design above. Then you could observe the robot interacting with its typical environment. You then could change to its design, for example, reducing its bumping into things or experimental random changes in the design to see what the change in per-formance will be. Developers of self-improving robots claim that they produce sophisticated robots that work as well as the ones designed by humans. Many examples and reports can be found by an Internet search.

Perhaps the most ambitious enterprise so far doing evo-lutionary computation to use computers to invent is Genetic Programming, Inc. headed by John R. Koza. They employ mutation, recombination and natural selection to achieve machine intelligence. Genetic Programming claims to have produced thirty-six inventions that can be categorized as competitive with what knowledgeable developers in the fields of application could do. Fifteen of the evolutionary technique duplicated patented inventions indicating that the genetic programming approach does have simple creativity.

It should be noted that these applications avoid having to deal with mechanical engineering, materials, fittings, etc., whose selection and optimization is the hard work of many inventions. This is consistent with my own experience with three patented inventions that involve chemical engineering, mechanical engineering and electronics all blended together. The Patent Office wants to see evidence that your creative insight can be reduced to practice.

The Genetic Programming, Inc. procedure essentially follows the six steps described above with some additional refinement of evolution and mutation. Their computer produced up to hundreds of thousands of genotypes that evolved over hundreds of generations. It can take a laptop computer a week or more to do the computations. Genetic Programming, Inc. expects that using 50 gigahertz workstations (very powerful computers tied to an online central computer), the evolutionary computation approach will be very acceptable for producing useful inventions.

A fundamental weakness so far of the AI invention process using genetic or self-improving algorithms is that it only works within a closed system. The program is given a list of components to interconnect and optimize, but so far, it does not allow inquiry into other methods or improvements to better achieve the invention's goals. It does not allow intellectual inquiry into all the resources, methods, and prior art found in the computer clouds. Eventually the automatic use of these cloud resources in the Knowosphere will become routine.

What Went Wrong with AI and Where Next

Human thinking is flexible and accommodates ambiguity, so strong artificial intelligence must include probability in its conception. It must look for patterns in masses of data. This development approach leads to structuring artificial intelligence based on biological models, like the human brain. We have been hobbled by our attempt to create intelligent computers, which operate by traditional step-by-step analytical logic.

Artificial intelligence presently works for smaller problems with more achievable goals. Successful applications include medical diagnostics, stock market trading, optimal vehicle control, mineral prospecting and home appliances. At best, there are AI controlled machines that can automatically do limited tasks such as vacuuming a floor or guiding a rocket.

The AI computers and systems up to this point have generally been judged to be disappointing in terms of the concept of devices that would mimic human thought and intelligence. It became clear that artificial intelligence programs were limited in scope because they incorporated step-by-step computational algorithms based on reductionist conceptions of how to solve problems. The models could not reach out and incorporate new variables or data that the model itself thought might be useful, let alone do anything abstract.

Further, the models usually did not assume that random changes in the situation from time to time could change the behavior of the system being modeled. For example, if we have a model of sunlight affecting an insect, we must assume that on some days, there is no sunlight and on some days, the insect does apparently random acts of non-obedience to the model.

In other words, we will have to deal with the real world where almost any situation of interest for resolution by very intelligent machines will have hundreds or thousands of variables. These variables do not have static relationships. Their interrelationships are constantly changing with time.

It is like looking at the morning television newscast showing a live video of traffic seen from a helicopter. While the flow of cars is the same from day to day at commuter hour, we observe that the flow volumes on given roads change depending on accidents, weather, special public events, etc. To model this traffic flow so that it can flow more efficiently when controlled by an AI computer gets more and more complicated as we peel back the layers and find ever more variables. This is also the case when modeling climate change.

The human brain gets around a lot of this complexity problem by storing many patterns for future reference. In the traffic analysis example, the experienced helicopter pilot would have stored thousands of patterns and the associated information about weather and the many other variables. Without doing the time-consuming exact computations that a computer would do, the pilot would project his thoughts based on analogies with historical patterns. This is an example of associative inference where the brain thinks in terms of patterns (not variables) stored associatively (related patterns are stored together) in the neocortex.

So far, though, we really have not confronted thought head-on, whether it is done in a brain or a computer. David Gelernter, professor of computer science at Yale University, writes:

> AI has no comprehensive view of thought: it tends to ignore some thought modes (such as free association and dreaming), is uncertain how to integrate emotion and thought, and has made strikingly little progress in understanding analogies—which seem to underlie creativity.

Gelernter goes on to say:

Computers don't know or care what instructions they are executing. Switching applications changes the output, but those changes only have meanings to humans. *Consciousness*, however, doesn't depend on how anyone else interprets your actions; it depends on what *you yourself* are aware of.

One of Gelernter's constructs is the *cognitive continuum* where all information you receive and remember is cognitively connected to all other information you receive and store. It connects such reasoning as analytical thought, analogical thought, free association and creativity. These thought processes all are part of mental focus or concentration. Without this cognitive continuum, he says that AI has no comprehensive view of thought. Gelernter's comments are an excellent measure of how far AI has to go.

4

AI AND LIVING BEINGS

I ncreasingly, we will compare AI to various living beings. One reason is that AI may substitute for human brains like the motor vehicle did for the horse and the robobee could for the honeybee. Another reason is to see what capabilities are required for each sophistication level of AI device or robot. Also, these comparisons will be helpful for evaluations of energy consumption, resource use, and waste generated.

An important point in comparing AI devices with living beings, including humans, is that it is not presently practical to use measures of intelligence to compare robots to species or species to species. There may be no such measure. I propose to use something much simpler: If a robot or AI computer can do a defined set of tasks as well as a human, then it has "equivalence."

Equivalence, as I use the term, is not a very scientific measure, but it is very practical. It is like the creation of the term "horsepower" for machinery as a unit of work. James Watt, a Scottish engineer, first used it in the late 1700s to compare the work equivalent of steam engines with draft horses. The comparisons may not work very well for horse-drawn equipment versus gasoline vehicles in deep mud or baking deserts, but it gives a generally useful comparison of work capability. The human being, incidentally, when powering equipment, can produce about 1/10 horsepower for extended periods of time.

The Turing Test is often mentioned when discussing machine intelligence. A simplified description of the Turing Test is: If an AI machine and a person are both hidden behind screens in a room, and an observer communicates with both of them, the AI machine will be considered intelligent if the observer cannot determine which is the person and which is the machine. When comparing a robot window washer versus a human window washer this test would be of limited use. Assuming they both get the windows washed, we would be interested in cost, maintenance, reliability, and safety to any human involved.

Figure 1, Comparative Intelligence, compares some living things with AI devices of similar intelligence. The intelligence of a bacterium, by any measure, is not precisely known, but it is probably safe to say that it is at least as intelligent as the cruise control in an automobile and probably a lot more intelligent. Many species of bacteria and worms can move based on simple criteria, such as detection of nutrient. This is simple stimulus response like a thermostat controlling a furnace or a very simple little robot doing a repetitive simple task, based on a stimulus or sensed changes.

As creatures get larger with larger brains and more complex lives, their intelligence must incorporate large memory and reflective thinking in terms of themselves in a larger context. This is consciousness. Much has been made of it for explaining the apparently unique intelligence of humans. However, the well-known neuroscientist authority, Christian Koch, writes that consciousness exists in simple nervous systems.

Intelligence	Nature	Artificial Intelligence
Yes-no This-or-that	Bacterium Worm	Thermostat Toy robots
Several senses Simple decisions High mobility	Bee Mouse	Home vacuum robot Small military robots
Intelligent search Intelligent decision	Bird Dog Dolphin	Four-legged military "mule" Google driverless car
Sense of time Abstract thought Imagination Thinking in analogies Complex language	Human	Experimental AI

Figure 1. Comparative intelligence.

He says, "Even a worm has the vaguest sense of being alive." He goes on, "Any system that has even one bit of integrated information has a very minute conscious experience." This, he says, reverts to the philosophical doctrine of the ancient Greeks and others that mind is found everywhere and that this phenomenon is called *panpsychism*.

Bees and mice have much better intelligence than bacteria and worms. They have more senses including detailed vision, they can make simple decisions, and they have high mobility.

From here, we advance to the next level of intelligence, such as embodied by the bird, dog or dolphin. These animals all have intelligence that many observers feel includes significant consciousness. They can sense by sight, sound, touch and smell; they can recognize patterns such as particular peoples' faces; and they can, within limits, sort priorities. Animals cannot accurately categorize events over long stretches of time, nor can they plan by time sequences far into the future. It is highly doubtful that they can think in analogies, or communicate with grammatical language. Their emotions can include fear and anger but not empathy. If they have self-awareness is very controversial. I think they do.

What sorts of robots are comparable to these animals? One that has attracted a lot of attention is the four-legged LS3 "pack animal," designed to carry soldiers' gear and supplies over difficult terrain and through complex landscapes. As of 2014, this state-of-the-art four-legged mechanical donkey, made by Boston Dynamics, can carry 180 kg (400 pounds), follow a squad through rugged terrain, and interact with troops in a natural way, similar to a trained animal. It only consumes gasoline and is bulletproof except for the sensors on its head.

Another smart vehicle is the Google car. It looks ordinary except for a mechanical head sticking up to observe the surroundings. It actually is a cluster of 64 laser beams to 3D map the surrounding environment. The car combines these maps with high-resolution maps of the world to develop its moment-by-moment driving program. Needless to say, the car also is monitoring traffic lights, pedestrians, cars in front and back, etc. The car has driven itself all around San Francisco's steep streets and around Lake Tahoe. Actually, Google is testing more than ten cars. Estimates about when consumers can buy the self-drive cars vary from 2020 to 2030.

The Google driverless car is very intelligent because it can drive and maneuver according to mapped and sensed surroundings, and it can respond to changes received from a human rider. Undoubtedly, it will be able to have conversations with a human. The ultimate challenge would be to drive across the country, chatting with passers-by, refueling, and perhaps stopping to seek repairs. By some measures, then, the Google car and animals like the bird, dog, and dolphin could be classified in the same intelligence class.

On the other hand, the Google car does not procreate, nurture its young, or hunt in the wild for food. The animals and the machines overlap in intelligence, but are not the exact equivalent to each other. There is room, however, to put in the Google car a computer with human-like intelligence based on, for example, IBM's cognitive computer chip discussed in chapter 3. It is difficult to see where this development could end.

Even closer to the human intelligence is a computer program in Japan called Torobo-kun. This is an AI program, loosely called a robot, designed to pass the University of Tokyo entrance exam. In December, 2013, it passed enough subjects to be accepted in 70 percent of the nation's universities. The robot did very well in history where associating facts is important, and it did well in mathematics which requires strong concentration and fast and accurate calculations. Torobo-kun, however, received low grades in the Japanese and English languages, which were examined down to the morpho-syntactic and lexical levels.

As for a computer equivalence of the human brain, Ray Kurzweil believes that we are getting close now by either of two approaches discussed in the previous chapter. In his 2012 book, *How to Create a Mind,* he writes that using the IBM cognitive chips that replicate neurons and synapses, a neocortex will be created with 10 billion neurons and 100 trillion connects. This is close to the capacity of the human brain and, notably, might use only one kilowatt of power—similar to a household appliance.

The alternate approach is to use high-speed supercomputers. Their circuits are over 10 million times faster than the brain's circuits, but the digital computers are not massively parallel in their computation structure. Kurzweil writes that to functionally simulate the brain, 10^{16} (10 quadrillion) calculations per second would be required. This is in range of the fastest supercomputers, such as Japan's K Computer, which, however, also consumes 10 megawatts of power—more than 1,000 homes.

Understanding the brain and developing similar computers should make a lot of progress over the next ten years. This is the goal of the European Human Brain Project comprised of 130 research European research institutions. It will employ leading neuroscientists, doctors, computer scientists and roboticists across the six research platforms of neuroinformatics, brain simulation, high-performance computing, medical informatics, neuromorphic computing and neurobotics. The project budget is $1.5 billion.

The research and understanding of the brain must not lose sight of the basic unique human thinking attributes including language, envisioning the far future, and empathizing with other people. Then there is free association, creativity, thinking in analogies and imagination. Finally, there are dozens of emotions which can flip the human thinking process from one general line of pursuit to another. I argue in my book, *MegaMinds: How to Create and Invent in the Age of Google,* that all those functions can be realized in the associative inference model of the mind. This probably can be realized with the neuronal cognitive chip technology discussed previously. Figure 2 compares humans and AI at the present AI state-of-the-art. It includes some practical trade-offs that I have not mentioned so far. Robots only need one source of energy and food, usually electricity such as from solar cells. They do not fatigue or fall victims to diseases. And they don't poop.

Advantages of a human	Advantages of AI
Abstract thinking	No need for food or water
Complex and flexible communication	Creates little or no waste
Sense of wonder and beauty	Usually needs only electric energy (e.g., solar)
Imagination and creativity	Does not fatigue
Emotions	Relatively environment insensitive
Can reproduce	Not disease sensitive
Can repair itself and others	
Disadvantages of a human	**Disdavantages of AI**
Needs food and water	Generally cannot reproduce or fix themselves
Creates waste	No creativity or imagination
Craves non-food, non-task consumption	Fabrication consumes common resources
e.g., games, debate, chatter	becoming scarcer like copper and rare
Fatigue	elements
Emotions	
Environment and disease sensitive	

Figure 2. Comparative advantages.

Consciousness and abstract reasoning are probably the biggest bones of contention when discussing AI. Certainly, anything from an automatic robobee to an automated battle tank requires consciousness of its surroundings in order to do its tasks. This may not be the deep and somewhat mysterious consciousness associated with human thought, but, like Google car, it is mapping the space it finds itself in. The incoming information is related to previously stored information about the area, and referenced to the work to be done. It could be as simple as the robobee sensing a blossom and moving towards it. The key, as AI pioneer and expert, Professor Marvin Minsky, has said is to restrict the robot's task definition to one that is useful and not overwhelming. So let us look at some robot applications that are already done now either in the field or experimentally:

Home and family
Vacuum floors
Wash windows

Cook food
Do laundry
Educate, amuse and watch the children
Play board games
Outdoor sports
Attend patients in nursing homes
Drive vehicles
Maintain the lawn and gardens

Commercial and Professional
Process insurance and other forms
Medical diagnostics
Part of team surgery
Accounting
Law research
Cook and serve fast food
Write news, novels and music
Call center services

Outdoor
Carry infantry supplies and equipment
Destroy jellyfish
Lift and transport heavy loads
Autonomous farm vehicles
Remove weeds in crops
Fruit and vegetable harvesting
Play soccer

Manufacturing
Manufacturing using 3D printing
Light assembly such as cell phones
Heavy equipment assembly such as cars

Factory specialty tasks
Warehouse order processing
Paperwork and accounting of all kinds

Once we see that the application of robots to single tasks that are well defined is becoming routine, the next step is to see how robots can be made more intelligent. Think of the process like the evolution of species.

First, we have to make the most popular models in the millions in order to reduce costs and include exotic materials and subsystems. For example, unusual circuit chips like the IBM neuronal chip that I have discussed earlier can only be justified by high volume production. This is no different from the mass production process Apple started to make cell phones and tablets. The larger robots would eventually be manufactured in similar scale to appliances and cars. The designs of these mass produced robots, however, have to be perfected through iterative cycles of design or redesign, manufacturing, customer response, and redesign. This is machines evolution at work.

Then the brains of these mechanical creatures must be improved with new knowledge and needs. Again, the analogy with cell phones and tablets applies. New applications and software improvements can be digested into the robots by downloading these software packages just like apps and updates are downloaded into phones and computers. As is done in those devices, a lot of the device's software could be stored in the clouds to be retrieved only as required. It is not inconceivable that what started out as a relatively simple robot could evolve through software upgrades from a worm to a mouse to who knows what? Maybe human in intelligence.

5

THE QUIET INVASION OF AI AND ROBOTS

When we project the composition and dynamics of the future ecosystem—say in 2050—we will have to include analysis of the impact of AI and robots because they will definitely be a significant part of the economies of industrial nations. They will change the ways humans work, think and communicate, and they will probably be a major force for reduced fertility and thus lower populations.

Automation, computerization, robotization—these and other terms are used to mean the same thing: The use of computer-based technology to do tasks that were previously done by humans. In some cases, as I have discussed about honeybees, the substitution extends to animals. We all know that replacing living things by inanimate computers can be done, but what are some specific examples of success that show the way of the future?

Invading the Factories

About six million manufacturing jobs in the United States have disappeared since 2000 according to Adam Davidson writing in the *New York Times*. That's about one third of the manufacturing sector. While many of those jobs were sent overseas, even more were lost to AI and robots. So far, there hasn't been a lot of debate or protest about this development.

In another *New York Times* article, John Markoff reports that at a Philips Electronics Factory in The Netherlands, 128 robots assemble electric shavers. They work day and night, 365 days a year. The management of that factory is confident that their robots can make any consumer product.

You may well think, however, that the Chinese will always do things by hand. They have hundreds of millions people to employ. Not necessarily. Terry Gou, the chairman of Foxconn, the Taiwanese electronics manufacturer whose clients include Apple and who has over one million employees, said, "As human beings are also animals, to manage one million animals gives me a headache," Markoff reports. A similar Chinese contract electronics manufacturer, Hon Rai, plans to replace 500,000 workers with robots over the next three years, according to Jane Wakefield at *BBC News*. Globalization includes robotization.

Established applications of manufacturing robots include automobile assembly and moving inventory in warehouses. Early adopters were manufacturers with large capital equipment budgets and in-house maintenance departments. Ford used more than 700 robots to manufacture the 2013 Escape model in Louisville, Kentucky.

The use of manufacturing robots will be increasing elsewhere with users ranging from mom-and-pop shops in the conservative U.S. rustbelt to large manufacturers in the third world. Who would not want to increase throughput, lower per unit cost, increase the reliability of the manufacturing process, and have fewer human problems?

One development of special interest for the smaller manu-facturers is Baxter, a 1.8 meters (6 feet) tall 136 kg (300 pound) robot. The $22,000 robot has two arms with grippers that can be trained to do what has been so far manual work on the assembly line. Baxter can be programmed or trained by an assembly line worker and can work alongside coworkers. It has grippers with interchangeable fingertips that act like a hand. They pick up objects exerting enough force so the object will not drop but not enough to break it. The robot can identify objects in various orientations and almost lost in a pile of other objects.

Rodney Brooks, Director of MIT's Computer Science and Artificial Intelligence Laboratory, founded Baxter's maker, Rethink Robotics, in 2008. He believes Baxter will be most widely used for:

- Materials handling. Counting, orienting and moving objects.
- Loading and unloading assembly lines.
- Inspecting, testing and sorting.
- Operating machines. Putting a part in a machine, actu-ating the machine's function, and removing the part.
- Packing and unpacking bags, boxes and trays.
- Light assembly. It can be quickly trained to snap parts together and put them in containers.
- Finishing. Grinding, polishing and other finishing operations.

These are applications common to almost all light manu-facturing companies, so the future bodes well for the Boston-based company.

A Danish competitor to Rethink Robotics is Universal Robots. Their robots are about the same price as Baxter but they have only one arm. They work faster, however, and can carry heavier loads. As of December 2013, Universal Robots has sold 2,500 robots and are greatly expanding their manufacturing capacity.

In one U.S. company, which manufactures valves, the Danish robots are moved to CNC (computer-numerical-controlled) metalworking machines, assembly lines and tube benders, as required. CEO Geoff Escalette notes:

"Our CNC machine normally produces 400 valves per month with two shifts, so we would have been forced to buy another machine even if we put a third shift on. With the higher run-rate using the UR5 robot, none of this was necessary." Shane Strange, his Automation and Integration Specialist, added, "If you can write a to-do list, you can program this robot."

On the lower end of the parts size scale, a hearing aid company is using the Danish robots to take parts as small as one millimeter (.04") out of a mold and assemble them into the hearing aid. A technician programs the robot for a task by showing it the movement pattern.

These small manufacturing robots and other small robots used in surgery, law enforcement, science and other applications are called "professional-grade service robots" by the International Federation of Robots (IFR). They estimate that the small robot sales will increase from 16,000 units in 2013 to 94,800 in 2016. This is a growth rate of about 80% per year!

Small Robots and Education

The "Personal Robots" category is the important bubbling, boiling caldron for tomorrow's robot industry. This is where many of tomorrow's robot entrepreneurs will start. For new low-cost robot product development, one must think of Steve Jobs who started Apple in his garage, building upon simple computer products that were then available but which were not user-friendly.

Smaller and cheaper than the service robots, personal robots are a variety of robots for consumers, research and education. Mass produced robots for consumer use including cleaning, lawn mowing, entertainment, hobbies and small research projects recorded sales of about 3 million for 2013, and their sales are expected to grow 20-50% annually according to IFR.

Exposure to "robotology" begins in preschool. The tiny tots can start with commercially available robots designed for them. One such robot is called Romo. He (his marketers have declared his gender) is a roving base using bulldozer-like tracks. An iPhone programmed with the desired app is slid downwards into a slot in the roving base. Romo can move towards a selected color, such as following a red ball; it can follow a line on the floor; or it can recognize a face using the iPhone camera and snap pictures. Needless to say, Romo will respond to commands from a computer, even via the Internet.

When the child has progressed into grade school, he or she can move on to the LEGO robot education pack. This has the parts to make motors and sensors for their robots. They are at the starting point to build robots of their own design.

As children move into high school, they increasingly are offered the opportunity to build a robot from scratch, often as a member of a design team. These teams pit their robots against the robots of other schools in what is often called a "robotic challenge." Their robots are less slick and commercial than those they experimented with when they were younger, and more often they are a lot of parts bolted together with the addition of a nest of wires and a circuit board.

When the students move on to colleges and universities, they can often find robotics courses both in engineering and other fields of study. As of 2013, twenty-nine colleges and universities offered programs concerned with the design, construction and operation of robots, and twenty-four offered robotic engineering degrees. This surge of offerings is fueled in part by the demand for qualified robotics engineers. According to the U.S. Department of Labor Statistics, the openings for these new age engineers will grow by as much as 13% annually through 2018.

Invading Offices

Friona fell 10-8 to Boys Ranch in five innings on Monday at Friona despite racking up seven hits and eight runs. Friona was led by a flawless day at the dish by Hunter Sundre, who went 2-2 against Boys Ranch pitching. Sundre singled in the third inning and tripled in the fourth inning ... Friona piled up the steals, swiping eight bags in all ...

A computer program called Quill wrote this. According to its owner and master, Narrative Science in Chicago, "Quill applies complex and sophisticated artificial intelligence algorithms that extract the key facts and interesting insights from the data and transforms them into stories. The resulting content is as good as or better than your best analyst, and is produced at a scale and speed only possible with technology – technology that is now patented."

The writing part of almost any information-processing job that can be reduced to algorithms can be automated. The AI analysis and writing programs will invade journalism, law, corporate communications, science, government, the military, novel writing and much more. The barriers were already breached long ago by software programs that analyze massive amounts of numerical data and reduce them to digital reports and files. One can hope and presume that fewer trees will be sacrificed because there will be less paper processed.

Customer service and call centers is an area ripe for automation. BMW uses an artificial intelligence program from London Brand Management to help launch its new fully electric car, especially to the United Kingdom's sophisticated high-tech community. Users text or type in any question in plain language about the car, and they are answered within five seconds.

If two other elements are added, automobile sales and support organization will shrivel to a few people. One is voice communications with the friendly computer. That technology is already available in hand-held computer phones and tablets made by Apple, Google and others. The other is massive data storage and analysis about customers. An example of this is IBM's Watson computer discussed in chapter 3. IBM has turned it into a robot call center. It uses IBM's Big Data Analytics to make sure the customers get the best answers for each caller individually. It analyzes what every caller says—you could say that it "listens and pays attention" better than many humans could. Like a human, it may not understand the question, but it does not put you on endless hold.

Estimates appear in the press and Internet about the obsolescence of white-collar workers to AI and robots. Typically, these vary from 40% to 70% by the end of this century in the United States. Whatever the number is, it will be large and provide a challenge for parents and educators in preparing tomorrow's youth for satisfactory employment. This will be discussed in detail in the next chapters.

Care-Giving Robots

While robots are invading manufacturing, they are creeping into the institutions of childcare and eldercare. People seem to accept robots as companions faster than professional caregivers might have thought.

Children have been candid about why they accept robots as companions. Sherry Turkle observes in her book, *Alone Together*, that:

"I have watched three decades of children with increasingly sophisticated computer toys. I have seen these toys move from being described as 'sort of alive' to 'alive enough'…Sometimes the question becomes more delicate: If a robot makes you love it, is it alive?" She continues, "Children were comfortable with the idea of a robot as both machine and creature."

Having crossed this barrier, robots are promising as caregivers.

Among the first of the children's robots and still the most enduring design is the Furby. This elementary robot is a ball of fur with bug ears and bright, inquisitive eyes. It stands 20 cm (8 inches) high and weighs about ½ kg. (one pound). The product was launched in 1998, and tens of millions have been sold. They are available in Wal-Mart, Toys "R" Us, Amazon and other retailers at prices ranging from about $15 to $70. Amazon gushes with enthusiasm about what a Furby can do:

Time to dust off your FURBISH dictionary because FURBY is back and ready to take the world by storm! And you better be prepared because FURBY has A MIND OF ITS OWN. Feed it, speak to it, tickle it, play music for it and shake, tilt or turn your FURBY upside down. But be warned—how you treat your FURBY will shape its personality! Are you ready to handle a FURBY?

FURBY has a MIND OF ITS OWN. You see, FURBY has likes and dislikes just like you. You will discover them as you get to know one another.

FURBY responds to other FURBYs. Introduce your FURBY to other FURBYs and see what happens. Again, you never know how your FURBY will react, so it may get along well with some FURBs and may have a bad attitude with others.

When you first meet your FURBY, it will speak FURBISH. But the more you play with FURBY, the more English it will start speaking.

A more intellectually advanced robot for children is Play-i. These colorful robots are not only fun to play with, but they can teach kids computer skills according to the Silicon Valley startup, founded by engineers from Google, Apple, and Symantec. The robots are adorable plastic creatures programmed and controlled by an iPad. The idea of using robots to teach kids programming, math concepts, and problem solving was started by MIT educator Seymour Papert who demonstrated the possibilities of hands-on learning with his *Logo Programming Language* and mobile machines known as "turtle robots."

Parents have shown interest in robots for children as baby sitters. As a practical matter, they are "always there and always ready." Turkle observes, "Children who have incompetent or boring babysitters are interested in robots. Those who have good babysitters would rather stick with what they have."

•••

There is a lot of interest building in robot care for the elderly. With the family disappearing from its traditional role of elder care, technology of some sort will have to be used to help the elderly. The challenge is enormous. Worldwide, in 2050 there will be 1.5 billion people over the age of 65.

An opening wedge is the robot always being there and always ready. Will grandmother remember to take her pills? Has she fallen and can't get up and call for help? Would she like a fuzzy, adoring, intelligent companion that requires less upkeep than a dog? Call Acme Robotic Home Care today!

According to a Georgia tech news release,

Robots are also being developed as household helpers. Georgia Tech's Healthcare Robotics Laboratory has experimented extensively with a life-sized robot, called PR2 (maybe he knows R2D2!). They wanted to see if the robot can help older adults sustain independence in their own homes. PR2 costs $280,000 as of this writing and its battery only lasts two hours, but the research and development has to start somewhere.

Participants, ages 65 to 93, viewed a video of the PR2 robot in action, followed by a written survey and structured group interview. The study results showed that robots were preferred over human helpers in 28 of the 48 identified home-based tasks. Cleaning kitchens, bathrooms and windows were all jobs willingly handed off to robots. Respondents were less preferential toward their artificial assistants when it came to sorting mail, laundry and washing dishes—the latter presumably because the robots might stop working if they became wet.

The Japanese are experimenting with robots in nursing homes. They have started with Paro, a therapeutic robot. The first version looks like a furry white seal. It costs $5,000 and reduces patient stress, improves their relaxation and motivation, and improves their sociability with each other and caregivers. A second version of Paro looks like a full-size human and can have simple conversations and play games.

A different kind of robots for nursing homes and other health care applications features video screens that connect health care professionals with their elderly patients. These telepresence robots might also take vitals measurements.

The Japanese government has a plan to develop robots specifically for elderly patients. One will lift and move patients and another will track dementia patients. Present experimental robots for the elderly cost about $200,000 each, but through mass-production, they hope to get the cost down to about $1,000. The Japanese had a shortage of 700,000 nursing care workers in 2010 and they estimate they will need 4 million workers in 2025, according to the Health, Labor and Welfare Ministry.

Japan finds itself a leader in dealing with care of the elderly with or without robots. A major reason is that its population is shrinking and by 2060 is projected to be about one-third less than it is in 2013. There will be fewer productive workers supporting an ever-growing retirement population. This trend is developing in more and more countries in the industrial world.

Making Low-Cost and Easy-to-Use Robots

The iPad and other tablet computers showed that a very sophisticated computer could be built on one circuit board. All the parts probably totaled less than $100. Anything that you needed that was not on the circuit board was available online from the Web or in the clouds. Accessible resources included additional software, more data, data storage, and reference information. I venture to say that for the large majority of future robots, a computer with the capability of the iPad will be able to satisfy substantially all the computing, sensing and control requirements.

I refer to the vast middle-swath of robots that will be used in retail, health care, light manufacturing, the military, agriculture, household chores, and so forth. I am not talking about the outlier applications like competitors to human intelligence doing very smart things, or smart fur balls for children.

Robot computer performance, of course, will increase as has everything else in the data world, approximately according to Moore's Law. Named for Gordon E. Moore, a co-founder of Intel, it says that the number of transistors in an integrated circuit chip double approximately every two years. In lay computer user terms, this is often interpreted to mean that computer power for the latest version of a given configuration, such as a tablet, doubles every two years.

A more difficult design task is to lower the cost and increase the user friendliness of the mechanical systems of robots. To minimize this problem when I was designing instrumentation for the plastics industry, I always searched for mechanical parts that were designed for other applications but would work in my equipment. The design and tooling cost of these parts had been written off, and they were mass-produced. As time goes by, the robot industry will develop standard mass-produced parts—fingers, for example—that can be manufactured cheaply and sold to all companies in the robot industry.

•••

As robots become widespread, they are going to replace millions of workers. These robots depend on people for their existence and increasingly we will see that the remaining population will depend on robots. This symbiotic relationship constitutes a niche ecosystem which will we will explore further as the book goes on.

First, we will explore the effect robots will have on jobs, and possible consequences for birthrates and population dynamics.

PART 2

SOCIAL PROBLEMS AND REACTIONS

EMPLOYMENT CONSEQUENCES OF THE AI AND ROBOT INVASION

We cannot predict accurately how the future will look in the robotized economy of tomorrow, but we can test the reasonableness of proposed scenarios. For a start, let us sit in on a job interview in 2050. Our heroine has just graduated from her local community college with a business degree and technology studies. This is her version:

I found my way through an ordinary looking office to a chair facing a desk and a nattily dressed roboperson sitting behind it. He spoke first, breaking the silence.

"Good morning, Amy," he said, smiling reassuringly. "Can I use your first name? We want you to feel part of our family."

"Yes, sir," I said, fidgeting. This Robot was more imposing than the ones we had to clean the house, cook, and wash the dishes.

"Let me get to our business. We have three job openings that might interest you."

"Oh, what are they?" I said. "I haven't received any summary information."

"The first one on the list is quite physical. You will be trained to remove factory robots that require maintenance, and you will move in substitutes and install them"

"All by myself?"

"Occasionally a handy man will be found to help, but most of the time you will use a helper robot. He can lift 250 kilos (550 pounds)."

"Hmmm. What's the second position?"

"You will assist a team of robots who are servicing cars and light trucks. You know, they are removing and replacing tires, doing lube jobs, and testing and replacing various parts. You will greet customers, help the robots find parts which tend to get scattered around, and help the AI computer order more parts."

"These positions sound interesting, but do you have anything, shall we say, more cerebral?"

"Well, here's one a little different. Do you have some familiarity with electronics and can you do delicate hand work?"

"Yes," I answered attentively.

"There's an opening to apprentice repairing robobees."

"Huh?"

"These fascinating little bugs are about three centimeters long and are programmed to pollinate fruit and vegetable plants and trees. They get banged around a lot, and a skilled technician must constantly replace their delicate wings and other parts. You might even get some free honey." He smiled, quite pleased his remark.

I thought for what seemed like a long time, and decided to probe further. "Do any of these positions offer a career path, so that I could reasonably hope to run, say, a vehicle repair company or robobee pollination service company some day?"

Robots don't think for extended periods, but this one seemed to be. I guess seconds seemed like minutes to me at this critical point in my job search.

"Well," he said, "we can explore this, but I can't offer much hope. At best, it will be you and the robots in the corporate office. Robots seem to work best when they are managed by robots, and they are not paid. The owners are always looking for the lowest cost solution."

At this point, I felt that even though it might sour the interview somewhat, I should probe once more. "Then after I gain work experience with the robots, I should look for something where I work directly with the owners?"

"Bingo!" he answered.

•••

I have no doubt that versions of this conversation will become commonplace by 2020 and distressingly so by 2040. As David Von Drehle so succinctly put it in *Time,* "The root of our problems is not that we're in a Great Recession, or a Great Stagnation, but rather that we are in the early throes of a Great Restructuring." It is starting in Japan where the government has plans to install one million robots in Japanese factories by 2025, up from 370,000 in 2013.

In 2014, Bill Gates, Chairman of Microsoft, spoke at the American Enterprise Institute on the future impact of technology on the economy. He said that he feared "software substitution" and elaborated: "Technology over time will reduce demand for jobs, particularly at the low end of the skill set...20 years from now, labor demand for lots of skill sets will be substantially lower. I don't think people have that in their mental model."

How did we get here? Probably the most quoted current work on the big U.S. economic picture from the beginning to the present is by the Northwestern University economist, Robert J. Gordon: "Is U.S. Economic Growth Over? Faltering Innovation Confronts the Six Headwinds." This paper questions the assumption by many economists and most of the public that economic growth will go on forever. He says, "There was virtually no growth before 1750, and thus there is no guarantee that growth will continue indefinitely...rapid progress made over the past 250 years could well turn out to be a unique episode in human history."

Gordon's analysis links growth to three industrial revolutions:

#1 – Steam power and railroads from 1750 to 1830. It took 150 years for this revolution to have its full range of effects.

#2 – Electricity, internal combustion engine, running water, indoor toilets, communications, entertainment, chemicals, petroleum from 1870 to 1900. This revolution was more important than the others and was largely responsible for 80 years relatively rapid productivity growth between 1890 and 1972. It also produced significant enhancements to the quality of life through airplanes, air conditioning, and interstate highways.

#3 – Computers, the Web, mobile phones from 1960 to the present. Gordon believes this revolution produced only a short-lived revival between 1996 and 2004, although other economists disagree.

He concludes:

Even if innovation were to continue into the future at the rate of the two decades before 2007, the U.S. faces six headwinds that are in the process of dragging long-term growth to half or less of the 1.9 percent annual rate experienced between 1860 and 2007. These include demography, education, inequality, globalization, energy/environment, and the overhang of consumer and government debt. A provocative "exercise in sub-traction" suggests that future growth in consumption per capita for the bottom 99 percent of the income distribution could fall below 0.5 percent per year for an extended period of decades.

Nobel prize-winning economist Paul Krugman sees a different future. In his New York Times blog "Is Growth Over?" he says:

Consider for a moment a sort of fantasy technology scenario, in which we could produce intelligent robots able to do everything a person can do. Clearly, such a technology would remove all limits on per capita GDP (gross domestic product—the final value of all domestic goods and services produced in a year) as long as you don't count robots among the capitas. All you need to do is keep raising the ratio of robots to humans, and you get whatever GDP you want...in a sense we are moving toward something like my intelligent-robots world; many, many tasks are becoming machine-friendly. This in turn means that Gordon is probably wrong about diminish-ing returns to technology...Smart machines may make higher GDP possible, but also reduces the demand for people—including smart people. So we could be look-ing at a society that grows ever richer, but in which all the gains in wealth accrue to whoever owns the robots.

I agree with Krugman, but I also think economists tend to overlook as basic variables economic resources. Copper and petroleum, both key resources for the economy, essentially will run out during this century. There will always be some of each, but the costs of recovery are expected to climb to unreasonable levels. Substitutes can be found for both but the resources squeeze will be getting tighter. Also, starting with a trickle of environmentalists and now including the general public, we find more and more initiatives for sustainability, less unquestioning support of industrialization, and more emphasis on local production.

What this means for the degree of robot use is difficult to say, but I think in the long term it will engender the use of more robots and AI than otherwise would be the case. This is because robots efficiently consume energy. They do not consume food, water, or generate waste. They can work twenty-four hours a day except for maintenance. This will also militate towards lower human populations because, at least among the populous low-income groups, there will be even less future for the children and less income to raise them. This is already happening in Japan and South Korea.

●●●

Ultimately, the question is about jobs. Everyone from the poorest to the richest is wondering about future unemployment. Very important, from a social stability point of view, is how the future unemployment breaks out in the lowest, middle, and highest income categories. A lot has appeared about this in the press lately with most of the reports tracing their data back to a study in September 2013 by Oxford University. This study used "a novel methodology to estimate the probability of computerization for 702 detailed occupations, using a complex mathematical model they refer to as the 'Gaussian process classifier.'" What woke up the world is their conclusion that 47 percent of the total U.S. employment is at risk to be automated over "perhaps a decade or two." Although the study was done in England, the occupational work data came from the U.S. Department of Labor.

An important point the authors, Carl Benedikt Frey and Michael A. Osborne, make is that "While computerization has been historically confined to routine tasks involving explicit rule-based activities, algorithms for big data are now rapidly entering domains reliant on pattern recognition and can be readily substituted for labor in a wide range of non-routine tasks. In addition, advanced robots are gaining enhanced senses and dexterity, allowing them to perform a broader scope of manual tasks."

Other important points to bear in mind when assessing the "robot threat" is that the acceptance of AI and robots has greatly increased as more of the machines know how to listen and speak in plain language rather than relying on keyboards, screens, and tedious coding. New applications call for humans and AI or robots to collaborate in tasks. A commonly encountered example with AI is that in the replacement of supermarket cashiers by automatic self-serve checkout stations, a human assistant is available to assist at several checkout stations.

Figure 3 shows 21 selected occupations of the 702 listed in the Oxford study and the probability of these occupations to be taken over by robots. Virtually certain to lose out to computerization are telemarketers and cargo and freight agents. Emergency management directors and recreational therapists mark the other end of the scale with virtually no chance of losing their job to computers.

Probability that AI and robots will lead to job losses by 2020
(1 = certain, 0 = no chance)

Telemarketers	0.99
Cargo and Freight Agents	0.99
Loan Officers	0.98
Real Estate Brokers	0.97
Hotel, Motel and Resort Desk Clerks	0.94
Waiters and Waitresses	0.94
Accountants and Auditors	0.94
Technical Writers	0.89
Medical Secretaries	0.81
Bartenders	0.77
Librarians	0.65
Machinists	0.65
Commercial Pilots	0.55
Dental Assistants	0.51
Statisticians	0.22
Lawyers	0.035
Marketing Managers	0.014
Mechanical Engineers	0.011
Dentists	0.004
Emergency Management Directors	0.003
Recreational Therapists	0.003

Source: "The future of Employment: How Susceptible are Jobs to
Computerisation?" by Frey, C.B. and Osborne, M.A.

Figure 3. Projected job losses.

Frey and Osborne's model predicts that workers in transportation, logistics, the bulk of office and administrative support workers, and production occupations are at risk. These findings agree with technological developments. They were surprised to find that a substantial number of service jobs are vulnerable to AI and robots. They note that there is a growing market for service robots and declining advantage of human labor in the hitherto safe jobs involving mobility and dexterity.

As *Time's* David Von Drehle puts it, "If your job involves learning a set of logical rules or a statistical model that you apply to task after task—whether you are grilling a hamburger or issuing a boarding pass or completing a tax return—you are ripe for replacement by a robot." Alternatively, maybe you can hang on as a robot's helper like the airline agents who assist using the boarding pass machines.

In any case, workers and potential workers fled factory jobs for the lower pay, for example, of restaurant jobs. In the last half of the 1900s, where I worked in the industrial northeast labor was shifting from making things to helping other people eat and sleep. Fast food restaurants, motels, and strip-malls moved in to the vacant spaces left by vacated and demolished factories.

However, that was a career choice saving only a generation or two. As Erik Brynjolfsson and Andrew McAfee point out in *Race Against the Machine*, "How can so much value creation and so much economic misfortune coexist? How can technologies accelerate while incomes stagnate? These apparent paradoxes can be resolved by combining some well-understood economic principles with the observation that there is a growing mismatch between rapidly advancing digital technologies and slow-changing humans."

While there is no sure formula for job security, as I will discuss further in the next chapter, besides acquiring technical, social and computer skills, a person starting out now should be a college graduate if at all possible. The old saying used to be, "If you can't find a job, join the Army." In January 2014, the U.S. Army made it known that it is considering shrinking the size of the Army's brigade combat teams by a quarter and replacing the soldiers with robots. The Army would like to go from 540,000 soldiers to 490,000 soldiers or less a year or so later. That's at least 50,000 jobs lost.

If robots and AI should take over a substantial fraction of all jobs—even if fewer than the 47% of the Oxford study envisions could happen—they could become a part of the family of organisms closely associated with man. This would be hard to envision with the clunky machines shown making automobiles. But now that the latest generation of robots has personality, can move around and do things according to what they see, and generally relate to people in sympathetic ways, the idea isn't so farfetched. It is not hard to see that robots in the workplace or home could be considered living beings identified as one or more species of artificial life.

The public has already accepted this in two movies, *Robot and Frank* and *Her.* In *Robot and Frank,* a son gives a personable domestic robot to his father, an aging jewel thief who lives alone. At first, he disparages the robot, but the robot wins Frank over, and they become buddies as the master criminal and his amiable sidekick.

Her, a more recent movie, shows a lonely young man discovering a virtual woman who is really an AI computer program. The spend time together, explore each other's psyches, and eventually find themselves in love.

These portrayals of robots and AI are apparently subdued although they are actually more nuanced than the classic science fiction versions portrayed as Hal in *2001: A Space Odyssey* or R2D2 in *Star Wars.* People do not find it strange to buddy up with a robot or computer program if they offer something— especially love and understanding—in return. They could become the new version of pets. As pointed out earlier in this book, Sherry Turkle explores these themes in detail based on her psychological studies of children interacting with robots, noting the present models of buddy robots are judged by the children to be "alive enough."

So two things are really going on here: robots are taking over our jobs and robots are taking over our hearts and minds. To a certain extent, this has already been happening through the growing dependence on smartphones by some people, particularly the younger generation. People are developing a sense of intimacy and trust with these otherwise inanimate devices of metal, glass and electronics that exceeds that with other people.

In the Brave New World of the next generation, those who have good jobs and can afford the continuous company of robots may forget about the disenfranchised population altogether. The robots and AI may have taken over, but through the back door of our emotions.

7

THE CHALLENGE FOR EDUCATION

When we educate students to get and hold jobs in factories, stores, health facilities and elsewhere, we should remember that there is a chicken-and-egg problem especially when robotics and automation are involved. Manager: "I don't want to buy robots because there's nobody around here who knows how to deal with them." Student: "Robots are cool but super complicated. How will I know what to study to fit in with the new job openings?"

I myself was involved in the first wave of manufacturing automation and was confronted with the problems of education for it. In 1980, as I was turning 40, I was hired to run a failing machinery manufacturing company in industrial northern New Jersey. We made extruders for the plastics industry. These were about the size of a pickup truck, and the larger models cost about $250,000. In 1980, that was real money. The extruders were used to make plastic film and sheet, textile fibers, and pipe. The company was in a decrepit manufacturing plant that sprawled over half a city block.

When I arrived for my first day of work, I noticed employees peering at me through windows and around doors. The telephone operator—yes, the phone calls still went through a switchboard—welcomed me, and my secretary whom I had just met, welcomed me with fresh coffee. She was seventy-five or so, and had been with the company from day one. She served the coffee very graciously for both of us in fine china and a silver tray. She sat down and awaited any dictation I might have after looking through the morning mail. No smartphone, no emails.

All the bookkeeping was done by hand into giant green ledgers. Proposals and invoices were laboriously hand-typed and multiple copies were made on a cranked "spirit" duplicating machine. No laser printer here! The office staff shared dark, wooden, broken down furniture. Dust and dead flies covered the windows.

Engineering boasted a collection of 5,000 blueprints, each of which folded out to cover a large table. Only the chief engineer had formal education. He received a mechanical engineering degree from the International Correspondence School (now PennFoster) of Scranton, Pennsylvania. I remember that they always had enticing ads in *Mechanics Illustrated* and offered programs in engineering, air conditioning, auto repair, nursing, cooking, and many practical careers. The study process took a long time and was through endless correspondence, drawings and notes, and phone consultations. The chief engineer was the best machine designer I ever worked with.

Now correspondence education has been reinvented as online Internet courses. The top level, high-tech course instruction is given by Stanford, MIT, and others, through an approach called MOOC, meaning Massive Open Online Courses.

About twenty machinists, welders, painters and a shop superintendent staffed the manufacturing plant. The metal working machinery included milling machines, lathes, boring mills, saws and grinders; and these were mostly left over from World War II when this plant was hastily equipped to manufacture aircraft parts.

The machinists were equally old. Most of them emigrated from a devastated Europe after the war, and with their machinist skills, they wanted to start a new life in The Land of Opportunity. Their common language that required no translation after arriving here was reading blue prints. As Old World craftsmen, they took great pride in their work. One by one, they passed away, and it was my job as the General Manager to take their toolbox and company life insurance check to the widow. I would sit with her and say a few words, and she would try to break loose from her Polish, Italian or Hungarian in reply. Although none of the emigrant machinists became rich, almost all of them owned their houses, and they enjoyed a quiet, family-centered life.

After several years, I purchased the company from its corporate owner on a time payment plan and set about restructuring it to make money. The corporation had refused to invest money in a losing operation. Within weeks, I replaced the switchboard and operator with an automatic phone system, replaced some of the office workers with simple computers, and the plant machinery was sold. I contracted out the parts manufacturing to nearby machinery manufacturers who had CNC machines, and we did the final assembly and test. The plant machinists retired quietly because most of them were well into their 70s and were working as much for something to do as to make money.

This strategy worked for a while, and we made a small profit. When I looked at rebuilding our manufacturing capability, I ran into a brick wall when I tried to find machinists.

The older generation was gone, and the new applicants rarely had hands-on skills. All they learned was through books, and they wanted to stay in the air-conditioned and carpeted engineering department programming the manufacturing machinery. If I pressed these prospective shop employees further about adding to their existing knowledge by apprenticing in the shop, they invariably threw up their hands and said something like it would be better to flip burgers at McDonald's.

Maybe not for much longer. A startup company called Momentum Machines has developed a "burger-bot," to be the heart of fast food stores. A burger-bot will prepare the ingredients, cook the burger in 10 seconds, and serve it. "Our device isn't meant to make employees more efficient," cofounder Alexandros Vardakostas told Wade Roush from Xconomy. "It's meant to completely obviate them."

My experience in trying to modernize machinery manufacturing is being replicated all over the industrial world. Now, however, the managers are trying to replace CNC machine operators and parts handlers with robots. The reasons include cutting costs, but they also include less downtime and some say better product quality. Today's plant managers face the same problems I faced in finding new generation machinists and helpers who are willing to work on the factory floor.

In addition, the managers require that their new hires be comfortable with the shop robots, read and write proficiently, and be able to solve math problems. They should also know how to repair, program and maintain the robots. And these jobs must pay better than the local restaurants.

•••

Early in the 1990s, I decided to get out of the gloom and doom of the machinery industry and try something in the more upbeat electronics industry. I started a company to make electronic instruments to detect harmful gases. The timing was good due to rising environmental concern, and new circuit chips were just being introduced to make possible simple and efficient designs. I myself designed the circuits and mechanicals of the first models.

In this case, electronic instrument manufacturing, automation was easy to do. There was not a lot of heavy machinery and invested capital to replace. The major part of the instrument was its circuit boards. These are "printed" circuits with the components such as circuit chips, capacitors, and resistors soldered to the conductors on the boards. After the engineer designs the circuit, computer aided design (CAD) software, a form of AI, lays out the circuit as it will appear on the board. The circuits are the complex of conducting paths left after a copper layer on the fiberglass substrate has been chemically etched away.

First, a fixed robot called a pick-and-place machine works at dizzying speed to find and grab ("pick") each of the dozens or hundreds of tiny components, and place them with paste on their designated spots on the board. Then a wave-soldering machine flows molten solder across the circuit board to solder the components permanently in place. A washing machine cleans the board, and finally an automatic tester checks everything on the board to be sure it will work correctly.

These machines reduced the labor cost to make an electronic instrument to the point where we were cost competitive with Asian manufacturers. My $750 gas detector delivered to a customer in Tokyo, duty and airfreight paid, was often cheaper than similar products made in Japan.

My little company, started on the kitchen table, grew rapidly and was a much greater success than my much larger machinery company. I eventually sold it to fund a comfortable retirement.

As of this writing, Apple has announced that they are bringing some Mac laptop computer manufacturing from Asia back to the United States. With the latest automated electronic manufacturing, Apple found America to be cost competitive again. Still, trained labor is a problem. Steve Jobs, Apple's then CEO, is said to have remarked to President Obama that every foreign engineering student graduated here should have a green card stapled to his diploma.

•••

So how do we keep people gainfully and happily employed in this computer age? Germany has long had an education system known as "tracking" that produces the kind of employee I was looking for. The student is selected for a track in the fourth grade based on what long-term course of study will lead him or her to a good job. The lowest track is vocational leading to a job apprenticeship. The highest track leads on to college preparatory schools and university education. While Germany is a high cost-of-living country, it still manages to export products like machinery that many other countries have all but given up producing, claiming that they are no longer cost competitive. It seems that German industry is greatly helped by its well-trained workers and that their industry's success in turn offers more jobs.

The United States has scored low among the first world countries in both educational achievement and STEM (science, technology, engineering and math) achievement. Recent testing typically ranks the United States 10th—25th among developed countries. In 90% of U.S. high schools, there are no computer science classes. Meanwhile, the Bureau of Labor Statistics estimates that by 2020 there will be1.4 million new computer science jobs, but only 400,000 computer science students to fill them.

Recently, three new career and technical education school models have been introduced in the United States. These are:

Early-College High School (ECHS) Students complete high school and receive college credit. The idea is to have a climate of high expectations and strong academic culture. There is a heavy emphasis on project-based learning and use of computers. A lot are charter schools, which receive public funding but operate independently from the regular school system.

National Academy Foundation (NAF) Started in New York in 1982, NAF fosters partnerships between the business and education communities to prepare students for successful careers in finance, hospitality and tourism, information technology, engineering and health sciences. Employees of local companies act as mentors and engage students in paid internships.

Pathways in Technology Early College High School (P-Tech) Students go to high school for six years, and earn an associate's degree. The emphasis is in science, math and technology, and all students have a job wait-ing when they graduate. P-Tech schools combine high school, community college and strong corporate participation.

If there had been a school like one of these near my machinery manufacturing company in New Jersey, I might have been encouraged to stick with the business. As I increased automation in all departments of the company—including using AI and robots—I would have been able to find long-term employees who were not only up-to-date in technology but who also would have had the drive and edu-cation background to keep themselves, their equipment, and their company up-to-date.

•••

From the students' and later employees' point of view, they have to see how their investment in their education is going to pay off in terms of supporting themselves and their fami-lies. They could consult the MIT Living Wage Calculator, an online calculator programmed by Professor Amy Glasmeier at MIT. The URL is in the references for this book. A few benchmark earnings minimums in terms of a living wage are: Single person, $8.83 per hour; two working adults with two children, $24.63 per hour. In order to rise above a life-time of poverty and to stay employed, we can see from fig-ure 4 that a new worker should have at least an associate's degree and preferably a bachelor's degree. As of 2012, the associate's degree could expect to earn $19.63 per hour or about $41,000 per year. He or she would face the odds of employment just below the national average.

This leads to the national employment conundrum: If the wages are raised significantly, the number of employed may well decrease because employers will seek more automation or will move the jobs overseas. Moreover, in view of the devastating effect automation and AI are expected to have on mid-range office jobs (see the discussion and chart in the previous chapter), secure employment positions will have to be sought higher up the ladder. This would indicate that tomorrow's workers should have at least a bachelor's degree, preferably with fluency in a second language or other useful skills. Even a master's degree may become the middle class norm.

What will happen to the unemployed and unemployable? Their numbers will probably grow many times over what they are today. In one way or another, they are likely to become wards of the state. A guaranteed minimum income for everyone is the most commonly proposed solution, but it could become prohibitively expensive. This will be discussed in more detail in chapter 14.

Higher education institutions are not without their own problems, however. In an article he wrote for *Time*, MIT's president, L. Rafael Reif, said, "At a technology-intensive research university like the Massachusetts Institute of Technology, it now costs three times as much to educate an undergraduate as we receive in net tuition...Some wonder whether today's online technologies—specifically, massive open online courses, or MOOCs, which can reach many thousands of students at a low cost—could be an answer. I am convinced that digital learning is the most important innovation in education since the printing press."

DEGREE	2012 HOURLY EARNINGS ($)	UNEMPLOYMENT RATE (%)
Doctoral	40.60	2.5
Professional	43.38	2.1
Master's	32.50	3.5
Bachelor's	26.65	4.5
Associate's	19.63	6.2
Some College	18.18	7.7
High School	16.30	8.3
Some High School	11.78	12.4

Data are for ages 25 and higher. Earnings are for full-time wage and salary workers.
Source: Bureau of Labor Statistics, Current Population Survey

Figure 4. U.S. earnings and unemployment rates
by educational attainment.

Today, students from all over the United States and the world are taking MOOC courses through the Internet. Most at present are free and some offer testing and course credit. Leaders in the MOOC movement have been MIT, Harvard and Stanford, and now many public, private, and for-profit institutions of higher education offer MOOCs and other versions of online education.

While it is nice conceptually for students to live in the university environment and study in the personal presence of the great professors, this approach is becoming uneconomical both for the majority of the students and for the institutes of higher education. Increasingly, it will be this way or no way.

To gain the most from higher education, students will have to combine learning through MOOCs with some physical presence in the lecture halls, laboratories and field trips. The correct blend of these approaches will of course depend on the needs of the student, where he or she is located with respect to the university, and the requirements of their field of major study.

•••

If the invasion of robots and AI were the only major socioeconomic change facing us, probably education could solve much of the problem. It might take a generation, but eventually more people would be productively employed again. While the industrial revolution of the 1800s took many people off the farm, most of them learned manufacturing skills and were back to work again. The Sputnik crisis of 1957 when Russia launched the first orbiting satellite was a more dramatic jolt than jobs slipping away due to automation, and so American education systems were hurriedly revamped, and for decades it looked like the good life was assured. After all, we landed the first man on the moon and everyone had a color television and a microwave oven. Now we have the iPhone and social media.

But much bigger challenges than Sputnik are moving in. They are less dramatic than a shiny, beeping ball in space, but they can potentially threaten our very existence. These are consequences of the industrial revolutions, and include:

- Serious depletion of natural resources.
- Extremely hazardous air and water pollution.
- Climate change which will lead to the destruction of many urban, residential and agricultural areas, and the mass relocation of millions of people.

By 2050, these paradigm shifts plus automation unemployment will threaten collapse in most areas of the world. Curiously, robots may offer an unexpected help that I have not discussed so far: They are energy efficient and produce a minimum of harmful waste. We could be facing an extraordinary restructuring.

8

POPULATION AND FERTILITY ISSUES

The elephant in the room is serious overpopulation. It is a global overpopulation problem because we are essentially a global economy, and we draw resources from all around the world. Energy, food, water and critical raw materials are disappearing. Pollution is increasing. But there is a glimmer of hope. As reported by Eduardo Porter in a recent *New York Times* article, reduction of atmospheric carbon dioxide caused by curbing population could mitigate climate change.

The North American countries, major Asian countries, and Europe are beginning to get involved with this problem in an unplanned and unexpected way. They are employing AI and robots for any application as soon as automation is technically and economically feasible. This could create massive unemployment, and for various reasons, population, already declining in many cases, could decline at an ever-faster rate.

We have seen in chapter 6, according to the widely quoted Oxford study, that robots could eliminate 25% to 47% of the jobs in the United States over the next twenty years. Of course, humans will work with some of those robots, and some humans will start new companies based on the applications of robots. So let's use the low end of that range and project that in 2035 there will be about 25% unemployment in the United States and most other developed countries. The situation probably will be complicated by untold numbers of immigrants pouring in, especially from the southern hemisphere, to escape the devastation of global warming and economic collapse in their less developed countries. Many of these immigrants will take most of the remaining bottom rung jobs.

It may well be a discouraging time to start a family. The well-off families will be very uneasy and probably almost all of them will live in guarded gated communities. Higher education will be very expensive, and the upcoming generation will be unsure about what to study, what to do, and where to go. Social endowment programs like Social Security and Medicare may be cut to almost nothing due to lack of funding. Resources will be seriously dwindling and climate change will be causing major damage. The United States could find itself with an authoritarian government like today's China or Russia in order to keep the peace and enforce controversial programs.

The Economy and Fertility

Thomas Robert Malthus (1766-1834), an English demographer and economist, studied and wrote about these issues two centuries ago. He kept looking for the links between population, economy, and the environment. In 1798, he published his defining work, *An Essay on the Principle of Population*. He thought that population growth would block progress towards a utopian society. Malthus is most noted for his view that population multiplies geometrically and food increases arithmetically, so that eventually mass starvation will set in.

There has been a debate about Malthusian ideas ever since, and Malthus has risen and fallen in acceptability by both the public and academics. His major theory generally has not had an opportunity to be empirically tested because, despite the world's startling population growth since that time, food production has kept pace through the adoption of scientific and mechanized agriculture. This enabled, in part, the Green Revolution that fed millions, especially in the Third World. In addition, Malthus did not foresee the greatly increased goods and services productivity due to technology and industrialization.

Malthus argued that population increases are limited by the means of subsistence, and that when the means of subsistence increase, population will also increase. The population increase will be limited by misery and vice. This line of thought lead to the "Malthusian Trap," named after him, stating that technological advances only result in more people and not in improved standards of living.

Today, with productivity increasing again due to automation, AI and robots, ever-larger numbers of relatively unskilled people are forced to accept subsistence jobs or unemployment. A difference now, compared to Malthus's time, is the advent of planned families and contraception. Enabled by changing societal mores, contraceptives, and more job and career opportunities, women are finding fulfilling alternatives to staying at home and raising a family. This can lead to dramatically lower birth rates. Declining population in both wealthy and poor countries is becoming the norm.

In 1960, Nobel prize-winning economist Gary S. Becker wrote a paper building upon Malthus' theories. It is a chapter in a National Bureau of Economics volume, called "An Economic Analysis of Fertility." He related the number of children desired in select U.S. populations to income, but he did not immediately see the positive correlation predicted by Malthus. Then he introduced the variable, "contraceptive knowledge," and a positive relationship appeared.

In 2005, Alicia Adsera, then at the University of Illinois, reported in her study, "Vanishing Children: From High Unemployment to Low Fertility in Developed Countries," declines in fertility rates corresponding to increases in unemployment (especially of women) starting in the 1980s. The International Institute for Applied Systems Analysis (IIASA) in Austria confirmed her findings in a 2011 report: "The recent global economic recession has brought an end to the first concerted rise in fertility rates across the developed world since the 1960s...A rise in unemployment and employment uncertainty was a key factor behind this trend."

As for the United States, in 2012, Jessamyn Schaller, then at the University of California in Davis, wrote a paper, "Booms, Busts, and Fertility: Testing the Becker Model Using Gender-Specific Labor Demand." Important to the demographic effects of onrushing automation, she presented estimates of the relationships between birthrates and local unemployment rates. The data was by state for all states from 1980 to 2005.

Schaller found that "fertility is negatively correlated with unemployment rates." It should follow that automation will indeed lower fertility rates when robots and AI become the principal cause of unemployment. She also found that whereas increases in men's earnings had a positive effect on fertility, "demand-driven improvements in women's labor market opportunities cause women to substitute away from childbearing."

If increases in unemployment and perceived lack of employment opportunity lead to fertility decline, then the remaining question is, "Does the massive adoption of automation and the consequent increase in unemployment lead to a significant decrease in fertility?" I suggest that the answer is a strong "yes." The Oxford study reference earlier certainly does not hold forth any hope of net employment increases equal to the jobs lost. The authors calculate that up to 47 percent of U.S. jobs could be lost in twenty years or so.

Major Population Declines in Asia

Populations already are declining in major industrial countries. These include Japan, South Korea, Germany, Italy and the United States (not including the increase due to immigration).

South Korea is a good case in point. That country's fertility rate dropped from among the world's highest at 6.16 births per woman in 1961 to a low of 1.08 in 2005. It is estimated to be 1.24 in 2013, still among the world's lowest birth rates. (The replacement birth rate is about 2.1 for most industrialized countries— the rate at which the population will stabilize—to as high as 3.3 in developing countries due to high mortality rates. The world average replacement fertility rate is 2.4 children per woman.)

Doo-Sub Kim, professor of sociology, Hanyang University, Seoul, South Korea, published a detailed study of the rapid fertility decline in South Korea. He notes: "Urban-industrial expansion has altered the utility and costs of children…the high costs of children provoked low fertility norms, values and attributes." The changing attitudes of women are of central importance: "Young South Korean women are well aware that their career and self-realization will have to be compromised once they get married and have a baby. Therefore, there has been a tendency among young South Korean women to consider marriage as a compromisable 'option' rather than a 'mandatory' process in the course of their life." He then goes on to generalize: "A similar explanation can be applied to the very low fertility of Japan and the southern European countries including Italy, where strong family systems are maintained." In his conclusion, Kim notes a factor that will become ever more important as AI and robots continue taking over jobs: "Since the mid 1990s, high unemployment due to a poor economy and an accompanying high sense of insecurity among young people have resulted in a delay of marriage and a decreasing proportion of those married which in turn, have affected fertility decline."

In Japan, which has a fertility rate of 1.46, in the same range as South Korea, demographers expect the population to plunge from 126 million in 2013 to 84 million in 2060. Now they are beginning to confront the additional concerns of climate change, resource depletion, and overwhelming automation. Kunio Kitamura, the head of the Japan Family Planning Association, commented that Japan "might eventually perish into extinction."

In 2014, Prime Minister Shinzo Abe increased the budget by $29 million for programs to boost the birth rate. Now local governments are organizing projects to encourage marriage and increase birth rates. Typical are coffee and cake matchmaking parties in cafes with piano music. Several hundred young men and women attend. If that does not work, what is next? Meanwhile Japan uses 250,000 robots in industry and expects to use more than one million by 2025, according to *Time*. Which is the cause and which is the effect?

World Fertility Rate Trends

Fertility rates of selected countries are shown in the "Fertility rates" figure 5. Contrary to a lot of U.S. public opinion, The United States, Mexico and India have about the same replacement rate and a little below the world replacement rate. While Asia accounts for about sixty percent of the world's population, it is also leading the population decline trend. All the countries with the most rapidly increasing populations are in central Africa, and observers say that these high rates may start to decline with the advent of wide use of contraception and the greater independence of women.

If Asia and Europe are trendsetters in modern family planning attitudes, with North America following cautiously, then we can expect the world's population to decline slowly. These countries, most of the northern hemisphere population, account for 78% of the world's population. The reason for a slower decline than apparent from the fertility rates is the "population momentum" or "population lag" effect. For example, for a population declining below the replacement rate level, fertility will continue to grow because of the high fertility of the previous generation produced couples who are now having children. This effect carries forward for several generations. On the other hand, the fertility rate for most countries may well continue to drop because of contraception spreading everywhere, greater independence of women, fear of lack of employment, and of growing importance, the discouraging atmosphere of accelerating climate change.

Selected Countries, 2013

Low rates, Asia	Singapore	.79
	Taiwan	1.11
	Hong Kong	1.11
	China	1.55
Low rates, Europe	Czech Republic	1.29
	Poland	1.32
	Italy	1.41
	Germany	1.42
Near replacement rates, large countries	United States	2.06
	Mexico	2.25
	India	2.30
Very high rates, Africa	Uganda	6.06
	Somalia	6.17
	Mali	6.25
	Niger	7.03

Source: CIA World Factbook

Figure 5. Fertility rates.

Figure 6, "World Fertility Rate and Population," shows actual fertility rates and populations for 1950-1955 and 2010-2015. We are now at a fertility rate somewhat barely below the replacement level, and the world population of somewhat over seven billion is close to a consensus estimate of the world's carrying capacity. The fertility could drop to 2.1 or so by 2050 when some demographers (but not yet the UN Population Division) expect the world population to stabilize. I feel, due to the recent influences on family planning discussed above, that by 2100, the fertility rate could be in the vicinity of 1.0—similar to today's South Korea or Singapore—and the world's population could fall relatively rapidly.

(2.4 is the approximate global fertility replacement rate)		
	Fertility rate	Population (billions)
1950-1955	4.95	2.5
2010-2015	2.36	7.1
2050	2.1 ?	9.6
2100	<1.0?	Decline starting as early as 2050

Source: Wikipedia: Total fertility rate

Figure 6. World fertility rate and population.

Population Sustainability

What is the world's human carrying capacity? What population is sustainable? Joel E. Cohen in his book, *How Many People can the Earth Support?* (called "the definitive work on global population" by E.O. Wilson), reviewed sixty-six models that have been proposed to answer this question. He found that estimates ranged from fewer than one billion to more than a trillion. Most of the estimates fall in the range of four billion to sixteen billion with a median value of 7.7 billion. This is close to the world's population as I write (2014). Cohen explains: "This enormous spread follows from widely varying concepts, methods and assumptions...These static and deterministic estimates are inadequate to picture human-planetary interactions that are intrinsically dynamic and full of surprises."

A further problem is that when many of these estimates were made, it was assumed that the developing world would not industrialize to the extent of Europe or America. Now representatives for the emerging countries say that they want to be as developed as anyone else is. This means that, for example, the production of basic materials like steel and copper will have to be greatly increased, as long as these resources last, and if the resultant pollution is not overwhelming.

Cohen's book was published in 1995 and in the nineteen years since we have become much more conscious of climate change, loss of biodiversity, and increased pollution. A book published in 2009 that is a wakeup call for these issues is *The Vanishing Face of Gaia* by James Lovelock. He is a climate scientist who sees climate and all other natural phenomena interrelated as essentially a living mantle on the earth, which he has called Gaia. While Lovelock's thesis is not universally accepted, his general vision of where the earth is headed is sound. He states: "There is no simple number for the carrying capacity of the earth for people...With science and technology present, the numbers are imponderable, and we have proved that 7 billion is possible for a short period. But how many will be in balance on an earth seven degrees hotter than now? It might be as little as 100 million if the carrying capacity of the land surface of a hot earth falls to ten percent of what we have now."

Why is all this important for this book? Now we must look at the pressures on populations and decisions about family size in terms of how AI and robots will change population size and trends. Within twenty years, the number of robots could be a significant population compared to other major species. They will have taken over many jobs that are routine, or, as engineers like to say, "can be reduced to an algorithm." This can be an advantage in terms of environment and resources because the robots typically will require less energy for a given task and will create less waste than humans who would do that task. Robots and AI virtual beings will also be companions for people and will be considered as family much as pets are today.

While the mechanical creatures are moving in, we are in the throes of a mass extinction of wildlife. According to E.O. Wilson, fifty percent of all the earth's species will be extinct by the end of this century. Even now, only ten percent of the big ocean fish remain. It will be devil take the hindmost, which could be man. That is why we have to know if there will be an overpopulation of people or if there will be a manageable and healthy population. Their numbers and the environment they create will guide how they interact with nature, natural resources, and robotic life. The results could be ugly or could be a bright new era.

9

THE AGE OF ROBOTS

The declining birth rates discussed in the previous chapter can be ascribed to concern about the costs of raising children, concern about reliable and adequate lifetime employment, decline of the family unit, and concern about the future, perhaps especially in view of climate change. Meanwhile, robots are moving slowly into most modern societies. We hear about an application here, an adoption there. The designs and applications of robots need to become more attractive. A day will come when almost every worker will collaborate with an AI computer or a robot, and almost every adult will have a robot to help around the house.

We will be entering a new world of transition over at least two generations. This will start with the young adults in today's "millennial generation" who are more excited about iPhones and cool social media than about automobiles and big houses. They tend to trust gadgets more than people.

Coincidentally, this attitudes transition will be about complete when Ray Kurzweil and others predicted the Singularity will occur—when computers will be more intelligent than humans. Not all computers will be super smart—perhaps only a few special purpose ones. Most important, by then, everyone will accept the idea that with a smart enough embedded AI computer, a robot will be able to do almost anything. I venture to say that it will be more important for a robot to have 1,000 application programs, or apps, than to have an IQ of 1,000. Better many faithful helpers in one robot package than just your own Einstein.

First Came Cars

The first American socioeconomic revolution was based on the automobile. Then along came television, which brought the world into our living room. Then there were smartphones, which serve as our portal to the Web and to our friends and connect us to the Knowosphere worldwide.

How well I remember the '50s and '60s. It was a time of anything-is-possible optimism which bubbled over to excitement about flashy car designs. The tailfins! The chrome! The white sidewalls! The four on the floor! This is irrational exuberance about cars, which has a certain value. The buoyant ads of the large American family, all smiling, going to the lake or beach in their "woody" beach wagon. This is what mattered when I was growing up. No more. Now cars all look the same as featureless shapes. They are all optimized for fuel economy and low cost. That is not a bad thing but not very exciting. In addition, they are made by robots. Soon they will be driven by robots.

When the first few automobiles were available in 1886, they were commonly referred to as horseless carriages. For the rich they were a new toy. Commerce latched on to the early light trucks as delivery vehicles. People were delighted to get rid of those horses that consumed a lot of expensive oats and indiscriminately pooped everywhere. This was the greatest revolution since the steam engine a century earlier.

According to a *New York Times* of the day, in 1910 the cost of using an automobile was $.0315 per mile and a horse and buggy $.0368 per mile. These figures included depreciation. The automobile was assumed to use five gallons of gas and one pint of oil per day, and the horse munched down twelve quarts of oats and twenty pounds of hay. The automobile's future appeared assured even in its less-efficient models. Twenty four million horses would become unemployed.

It was not just economics. Consider the environment. Eric Morris writes in *From Horse Power to Horsepower*, "By the late 1800s, the problem of horse pollution had reached unprecedented heights. The growth in the horse population was outstripping even the rapid rise in the number of city dwellers. American cities were drowning in horse manure as well as other unpleasant byproducts of the era's predominant mode of transportation: urine, flies, congestion, carcasses, and traffic accidents."

In 1908, Henry Ford introduced his Model T, which he kept in production until 1927. It brought low cost personal transportation to the middle class like Steve Job's iPhone did as everyone's personal phone about a century later. Nobody could foresee the effects of cheap personal transportation—sprawling suburbs, serious air pollution, and carnage on the highways. There are some surveys that reveal that young adults today may prefer an iPhone to a car, if they must choose.

Next comes the Robots

Will robots be a transformational force like the automobile? No one knows for sure, but we have seen that they could wipe out half our jobs and at the same time become lovable help-mates. Could robots be the basis of the next great socioeconomic revolution in modern American Life?

If we combine the mechanical genius of the automobile with the image transmission of television and the connectedness provided by the smartphone, we have the key components of the robots. They can be alive enough so we can care about them, and they can revolutionize our economy.

Like cars, television and smartphones, mass adoption of robots will depend on mass production to reduce their cost, and people-oriented packaging so that they can be as attractive and simple to operate as smartphones.

●●●

Robots and AI can also provide a huge package of benefits to people and may well be the next big thing. These benefits include:

- Do undesirable jobs such as weeding fields and picking crops.
- Work in occupations that cannot support the pay required by humans such as washing dishes in restaurants.
- Companionship for retired people and indeed for everyone.
- Consume less food, water and energy than equivalent humans and leave less waste in the environment.
- Can be controlled by smartphones or other simple electronic devices.

- No need for retirement programs, childcare, education, and other human services.

Robots still need further design improvements to make them as easy to use as an automobile. A lot of those improvements will require mechanical engineering, which typically has longer design, prototype, and test times than do software and electronic engineering projects. The automobile went through about fifty years of improvements before it became anything close to the reliable, user-friendly machine we take for granted today. Another product conceptualization and design challenge is that a popular robot should be able to do many tasks rather than forcing the user to buy a robot for each task.

AI in faceless, invisible computers generally does not have the mechanical engineering challenges that robots present. It does require, however, time for developers to discover, analyze and write software apps for all the applications commonly required.

The same is equally true for robots. For example, you can buy an off-the-shelf robot today to vacuum your floors, but will it also wash the windows? Currently there are very few robot apps and almost no universal application robots to use them.

Meanwhile, as of this writing, there are about one million apps available in the iPhone app store. These are not just music, but are mostly other applications including games, industrial procedures, and mortgage payment calculators. If there were only a thousand apps for robots including playing games with humans, their sales would take off.

An Emerging Large Scale Robot Industry

Google, the 68th largest company in the world in 2013 and one extremely tuned to having the Next Big Thing in transformative technology, has purchased eight robot companies at a cost approaching sixty million dollars. Their new Director of Engineering is Ray Kurzweil, who has been mentioned earlier as an inventive AI specialist and famous for his declaration of the Singularity.

This looks like a repetition of the first wave in personal computers, tablets and smartphones. Modern laptop computers became common in 1991. Apple released its first tablet computer, the Newton, in 1993 and the iconic iPad in 2010. They introduced the iPhone in 2007.

The other enabling development was Google's introduction of the Android operating system for smartphones and tablets. It is essentially a universal solution for technology companies requiring a ready-made operating system that they can modify to their special requirements. Besides detecting finger swipes, Android connects to accelerometers, proximity sensors, and GPS. As of late 2013, 71% of mobile software developers use it.

There is a promising future for Google robots, although there will of course be significant competition. They will combine their Android device language with their collection of robot designs from their eight robot companies. They have already developed robot experience and credibility with their self-driven Google car.

Meanwhile, Japanese Prime Minister Shinzo Abe announced in June 2014 announced that he would set up a task force to develop Japan's robot industry and triple the size of the market to twenty four billion dollars. He commented, "We want to make robots a major pillar of our economic growth strategy," and added, "In 2020 I would like to gather all the world's robots and aim to hold an Olympics where they compete in technical skills."

The race is on.

Environment and Energy

We have seen how tiny robots might take over some of the pollinating traditionally done by bees that disappeared due to CCD. In general, robots should contribute positively to both improving the environment and conserving energy. In the long run, if robots do well in both of those areas, barriers to their acceptance will fall.

Assuming the population declines, the amount of waste directly produced by humans, such as sewage, will also decline. The population decline could accelerate as robots invade more human occupations. Indirect waste production by humans should also decline. This includes all waste arising from human activity. An example is burning gasoline in cars and other machinery and producing carbon dioxide and soot in the process. Fewer people will mean less pollution.

Energy savings is where robots make big inroads. As of 2013, while doing a task, robots may use as much energy (kilowatt-hours or calories) as a human, the savings really add up when considering that robots use no calories when not working. Humans consume some energy all the time, even when sleeping or watching television. Further, robots generally do not require precise heating or air conditioning in their workplace.

Overlapping with the energy comparison is the fact that robots do not need food or water. By receiving energy as electricity from, say, stored solar energy, robots bypass the chain of creating vegetable foods from solar energy and photosynthesis plus nutrients from the environment. According to current studies, water soon will be the nutrient in shortest supply both for direct consumption by humans and animals and for growing grains, vegetables and fruits.

We will explore these topics in more detail in the next chapters.

10

ROBOTS AND ENERGY

The ancient Greeks saw the transformative significance of energy when they created the myth of Prometheus. He created man from clay and as a champion of humankind, gave humanity fire. The gods punished Prometheus for this grave error by having his liver torn out and devoured by an eagle. Prometheus was chained to a rock and his liver grew back every day, just in time for the eagle's daily visit.

Now our Promethean fire is fueled by oil, coal, nuclear and other energy sources. We in turn have been cursed with air and water pollution, mining deaths, escaped radiation, and climate change. Civilization as we know it is on the verge of life support.

The emergence of robots will change this picture at least somewhat. Large-scale automation should reduce the world's net energy consumption significantly. The effect will be particularly pronounced if populations of people drop rapidly at least in part due to robots taking over jobs.

Enterprises of all kinds will accept robots at an ever-faster rate when the robots are demonstrably cheaper than human labor, and when there is a perfectly working model for any given application. The robot producers have a long way to go in offering a wide variety of designs for all kinds of jobs. It is not that the engineers cannot produce great designs; it is generally more of a question of budgeting the time, people, and other resources to design for applications. Probably in ten years, the large majority of feasible applications will have robotic solutions available.

As automation takes over more jobs, and if the population declines partially as a result, there will be a significant reduction of energy consumption. This is partially because humans use far more energy each day than do robots.

Industrial and Commercial Robots

To start this analysis, I will compare the relative on-the-job cost advantages of robots and humans for various tasks. The engineers have conquered the robot cost barrier years ago. It is difficult however to predict true robot costs yet because we don't have a long history of data about repairs, obsolescence, the degree that humans should be working with the robots and so forth. Nevertheless, the comparative data of robots versus human workers is becoming clear enough so that we can make a useful comparative analysis as shown in the chart "Hourly Cost of a Robot vs. a Human" in figure 7.

Starting with the robot, I assumed a robot that would assemble small equipment and machinery. A typical manufactured product would be a power lawnmower. This equipment assembly represents a typical area where robots are taking manufacturing jobs. This robot is a medium-size industrial robot that can lift 100 kilograms (220 pounds) and consumes about six kilowatts. I assume a $30,000 price, which is probably high. I priced electric power for the robot at ten cents a kilowatt-hour, which is near to what a small shop would pay, although large plants would probably pay seven cents or less. Pneumatic power, such as for the grippers, is considered negligible by comparison. I estimated indirect cost at 2.5 times the equipment cost as recommended by the *Handbook of Industrial Robotics*.

	Robot	
Electricity	Indirect Costs[1]	Total Cost
$.60	$1.25	$1.85

	Human	
Wage	Benefits[2]	Total Cost
$15.00	$4.50	$19.50

1 – Includes tooling, maintenance, spare parts, downtime, and financing. Robot's price assumed to be $30,000 with a useful life of 10 years. Source: Various robot industry publications.

2 – Includes health insurance, retirement benefits, and paid leave. Source: U.S. Bureau of Labor Statistics.

Figure 7. Hourly cost of a robot vs. a human.

As for the worker's wage, I used an entry-level pay of $15 per hour, which is near the minimum wage in many areas. He or she could be earning 50% more if they were skilled and had a lot of job experience. I added normal benefits, which would be the case for full time workers.

The robot is clearly cheaper. How long will it take its savings to pay for itself? Taking Total Costs from the chart, we subtract the robot hourly cost from the human hourly cost and get a saving of $17.65. We multiply this by 2,000 hours to get the cost savings per year if they worked one shift, 4,000 for two shifts and 6,000 for three shifts. The $30,000 machine would be paid off in 10.2 months, 5.1 months or 3.4 months, respectively. These are in the range of robot industry estimates, which typically are around seven months, although assumptions are often vague and can vary widely.

We now can see that most routine robotic applications could be justified on a cost basis. Looking beyond the simple robot-for-person substitution, a skilled person, who typically did the work before robots were introduced, working with several robots would be cheaper per workstation than the same number of workstations with no robots. In addition, this human co-worker or "supervisor" would make the whole operation more productive than with only robots because problems can quickly be corrected and product quality can be perfected through ongoing adjustments.

Household Robots

Simple but effective robots are becoming accepted for home use. Figure 8, "Robots for the Home," shows three applications, the typical costs involved, and the time of use to pay back their cost, assuming replacement of a $25 per hour friend or family helper. The payback times could be even less for a $50 per hour professional, although they probably would bring their own equipment, saving the homeowner this expense.

In any case, it would only take a few vacuumings of the typical home or apartment for the vacuum robot to pay for itself. It would fascinate both pets and humans as it dutifully sped about the floor. Its success would lead to the thought, "Couldn't it be only a matter of time before robots for washing dishes and putting them away, and doing the laundry and folding it in neat piles become available?" They are indeed under development.

Some of the robo vacuums look like a large hockey puck and are about 38 cm (15 inches) in diameter and 9 cm (3 ½ inches) high. Others look more like a squashed electronic box, but the principles are the same. They are cordless and hoseless with a battery charging station, and the vacuumed dust is stored in a filter compartment.

These little machines do hardwood floors and all but deep carpet. They zip around under furniture. They know when they have vacuumed everywhere and automatically return to their charger. Some models can be programmed to vacuum automatically on a set schedule, and some have special features to vacuum in tight spaces and to vacuum more intensively in the dirtiest areas.

	Robot ($)	Conventional Equipment ($)	Payback time for robot (Hours)
Vacuum Cleaning	100-700	200-300	10-35
Window Cleaning	200-400	about 100	13-20
Lawn Mowing	1,000-4,400	200-800	50-220

Source: L. Kilham, 2014

Figure 8. Payback of robots for the home.

Window washing is another home and commercial chore with robots ready to do the job. These are fascinating creatures, about half the size of the robo vacuum cleaners. They travel around the window in a pattern they compute will optimally cover the whole window area.

Then there is the outside. While no new consumer product has come along yet to robotically trim trees, there are robots available to clean leaves and dirt out of gutters. These are about three hundred dollar creatures with bulldozer treads and a big rotating brush upfront. They should cut down on the number of accidents on ladders and clambering around on roofs.

People with swimming pools will appreciate offloading the chore of pool cleaning to a robot. These are about the size of a conventional vacuum cleaner and gain traction with wheels or treads. They crawl around the pool, up and down walls, and climb stairs in seemingly random patterns that wind up covering the whole area. The pool cleaning robots are typically $500-$1,300.

Robotic lawn mowers are very practical and can take over a large track of time of the homeowner or hired help. Some look like a toy space ship and others look like a little all-terrain vehicle. Prices range from $1,000 to $4,400. Regular power lawn mowers range from $200 to $800.

The robo mowers are powered by a rechargeable battery and, depending on the model, will mow from 1/6 of a hectare (1/16 of an acre) to 12½ hectares (5 acres) on a charge. All mower designs use a thin wire around the lawn to indicate to the mower that it is at the edge of the lawn. Some also detect objects in their path like feet and pets, and some will shut off if their handle is touched. Some mowers have child safety locks and anti theft PIN codes to prevent unauthorized operation.

How many household robots are there in the United States? About three million were sold worldwide in 2012 according to the International Federation of Robotics (IFA). A conservative estimate is that a third of those, or one million, were sold in the U.S. The IFA estimates that the average sales price was $400. Since this is a new business, unknown to most consumers, I estimate that one million household robots were already in place in the U.S. so that the total U.S. population of household robots was about two million as of 2012. The IFA calculates the current growth rate of the market to be 20% a year. In ten years, the household robot population could grow to almost eight million from the 2012 base.

The unemployment caused by the household robots is difficult to estimate. Some jobs will be created to sell, service, and operate household robots. Entrepreneurs and their employees will be buying some of the robots as the basis of contract home maintenance services. The unemployment created by household robots probably will not exceed one million in the United States.

Reduction in Energy Consumption Due to Robots

It should now be clear that for industrial, commercial and home use, AI and robots in most cases are significantly cheaper than the human labor they replace. Therefore, after a decade or so of phase-in, they should be making serious inroads in employment. While this is a major social disruption, it also has a beneficial side.

If the human population starts to decrease, and probably at an accelerating rate, the consumption of energy will fall correspondingly. See chapter 8 and figures 5, 6 and 7. The important consequences of this are that climate change will be slowed down or even halted, and environmental disaster may be averted or significantly postponed.

In a report titled "Global Demographic Trends and Future Carbon Emission," Brian C. O'Neill and colleagues summarized their research results as:

> Substantial changes in population size, age structure, and urbanization are expected in many parts of the world this century. Although such changes can effect energy use and greenhouse gas emissions, emissions scenario analyses have either left them out or treated them in a fragmentary or overly simplified manner. We carry out a comprehensive assessment of the implications of demographic change for global emissions of carbon dioxide. Using an energy-economic growth model that accounts for a range of demographic dynamics, we show that slowing population growth could provide 16-29% of the emissions reduction suggested to be necessary by 2050 to avoid dangerous climate change. We also find that aging and urbanization can substantially influence emissions in particular world regions.

That report was part of the *Proceedings of the National Academy of Sciences of the United States of America*, August, 2010.

Already, fertility rates in Japan, South Korea and many western industrialized countries are beginning to decline. This reflects a new sense of insecurity among young people due to money, climate change, resource depletion and overwhelming automation. In addition, the new generation of young women is increasingly considering marriage and family as an option rather than as an essential component of normal life.

How big could the "population effect" be? The best place to start would be with the unemployment predicted by the Oxford University study cited in chapter 6. The authors concluded that 47 percent of U.S. jobs might be lost to automation over the next decade or two. That would be 66 million jobs based on the approximately 140 million currently employed in 2014.

But we know from mechanical automation of the late 1800s and early 1900s, notably the development of farm machinery, that new jobs are created due to the new machinery and other jobs are created due to advancing technology in general. Many of the displaced farm workers went to work in the cities.

We have to start somewhere, so I will assume that half of the projected 47% of the workforce displaced from jobs is the net unemployment number. This 23 ½% or 33 million lost jobs. The other 33 million jobholders are accounted for by slower adoption of the automation than the Oxford study forecasted, some of the newly unemployed are retrained for other occupations, and there are new jobs created because of the automation: technicians, engineers, salespeople and others. The unemployment created by home robots, that I calculated to be less than a million, is very small by comparison.

The U.S. annual energy consumption for those people permanently unemployed due to automation is about 231 million TOEs. A TOE is metric ton of oil equivalent and probably is the most common international energy unit. (The metric ton is 10% heavier than the U.S. ton.) This is how much energy would be saved if the population eventually declined by 33 million people. It is about equal to the energy consumption of Brazil. Assuming the other major industrialized countries adopted automation with an eventual similar reduction in population, the energy saved could be over 800 TOEs or about half the energy consumption of today's European Union.

This good news must be tempered by the realization that the population drop due to fertility decline cannot happen in a year or so. It takes several generations to take full effect, so forty to fifty years must pass before the effect is in full force.

The United Nations Intergovernment Panel on Climate Change (IPCC) in a draft report in April 2014 suggests that to keep global temperature increases below 2 degrees C (3.6° F) by the end of the century, emissions need to fall by 40-70 percent by 2050. The robotics-caused population drop approaches the lower end of that scale. In any case, we can be sure that job reduction through automation, over the long run, will be very helpful in reducing the severity of climate change.

Forces of Reaction

As AI and robots hit home in everyone's consciousness, political reaction will start to build. It already has in the minimum wage debate. While low-cost offshore manufacturing has been the bad guy in wage negotiations, increasingly we hear about robot manufacturing or office automation taking jobs here and causing major layoffs there. The real pressure will be on when unemployment creeps up above 10%.

Under pressure from the voters, governments may well stall the unemployment damage of large-scale robotization to some extent either by offering major make-work jobs such as infrastructure rebuilding or by a living "wage" for everyone, even though many of the employed may still not work. But now with ballooning social security and eldercare costs, and no major cuts in military budgets, none of today's major governments will be able to afford those unemployment offset programs for long.

PART 3

ROBOTS AS PART OF THE ECOSYSTEM

HOW SMART DO ROBOTS NEED TO BE?

When there is less demand on the environment due to reduced populations, climate change may be much less severe. As a result, there may be a reprieve from the often-forecasted apocalypse.

For the balance of this book, I will describe how the transition to an ecology and economy with strong dependence on AI and robots will occur. We will explore the mechanisms underlying the new eco-economy, with emphasis on the information and intelligence factors involved.

•••

The change a species undergoes, from generation to generation, is determined by random genetic variations which survival determines to be improvements. While bacteria and fruit flies have very short generations, and evolutionary changes can happen in weeks to months, for large animals and plants, generations are measured in tens of years.

Humans in a basic sense are stuck with this same slow rate of species improvement. It takes roughly a hundred thousand years to evolve a discernibly better model of human. The futurists see overcoming this slow pace by modifying the human genetics and brain, and this may be demonstrated in a few dozen years.

Humankind has improved upon its genetically constructed brain and mind through the development of culture. Our information, knowledge, language, science, social constructs, art and all elements of culture have accumulated over the decades and millennia. We pass this on from generation to generation as an ever larger and ever improved resource. Our genetic evolution has not kept up, so we have used technology in its many forms to enable our goals.

Species with computer brains (their brains can be as small as a computer chip) leap frog that evolutionary improvement process because their programming is in their electronic memory instead of genes packaged into genomes. Changes in the algorithm or data can be made in the organism at any time and can be programmed to be passed on to the next generation of the organism. These organisms are anything with intelligence programs including AI computers, robots, drones, power plant control systems, and smartphones.

Of course, some new programming may require new physical design of a species of robot. Perhaps the new, improved robot should have longer arms or color vision. This gives people something to do!

At this point, people get concerned or even scared. "Won't the robots take over?" Where before, people did not think robots could be made smart enough to do the tasks expected of them, now the people imagine robots to outsmart human beings and take over. It is not going to happen.

Typical robots only need the intelligence and computer capacity of a smartphone, which is basically a small computer with sophisticated sensors, and control methods. In fact, future robots might use modified smartphone circuit boards for their thinking, communications and control functions. Hopefully, they will converse with their human owners!

•••

Someday, maybe in less than a decade, when there are millions of robots operating in the economy, directed by humans, how much intelligence will the basic robots need?

We can start with the derivation of the word "robot." It is derived from the Czech term for forced labor, "robota." Most of the robots likely to be used at work or at home fit that description nicely. These regular robots will not use sophisticated AI for complex problem solving. They will just tirelessly labor away.

Robots typically have a movable body which either swivels or it rolls around. These robots are designed to carry out a repetitive operation continuously such as welding, screwing on bottle tops, spraying paint, or assembling a group of parts. The robots in movies may look like humans, but their vertical two-legged construction can be unstable. Most industrial robots have an arm or two flexing from a central support, which may also have limited movement. Wheels or treads are generally used for home, military and outdoor robots.

The industrial robots often amount to a sophisticated hand, wrist, elbow, arm and shoulder. These are activated by Hydraulic or pneumatic cylinders, or motors. A simple computer panel controls everything after combining programmed control and usually optional external control. There must also be sensors. Depending on the task requirements, these sense position, obstacles, and parts often by infrared beams. The robots may also sense sound, video images, and movement and location.

None of the foregoing would indicate that the robot would need great intelligence. To describe the demands on robot intelligence, I have selected highlighting a robot that would interest almost anybody if they do not have one: a home robotic vacuum. Its degree of complexity is similar to a small industrial robot or a simple agricultural robot.

The Roomba is a popular home vacuum robot. We will look at their basic low cost model (about $150), the "Roomba Red." It is 33 cm (13 inches) in diameter and 9 cm (3.5 inches) high. The built-in rechargeable battery will power the robot for about two hours, roughly the time to do one room. This little vacuuming package has five motors: one for each of the two wheels, and one each to vacuum, brush, and "agitate." (Bring dirt in directly through a set of brushes.)

Multiple sensors and a navigation program are essential to the robot's success. These sensors are used to enter data to calculate the size of the room and to change the robot's direction if it is approaching a "cliff"—usually the drop-down entering a stairway or a lower split-level. The robot cleans by rolling around in a spiral pattern, starting from the outer edge of the room.

If the Roomba detects a large amount of dirt coming in, it will vacuum that area again. It also has a side brush, which it can activate to sweep dirt from corner areas into the vacuum inlet. When the robot decides that the room is done, it will engage its sensor to find the battery charger, and it will scoot over and dock in the device.

How much creature intelligence does the vacuum robot have? To my knowledge, there are no precise comparative tests, but it may be helpful to review the animal intelligence information in chapters 2 and 4. From those, I suggest that a small, special-purpose robot like the Roomba vacuum should have the intelligence equivalent of an earthworm.

The key criteria are that the robot only should have the intelligence necessary to do its job. This is of course for reasons of lowest cost, simplicity, and ease of use. Such an intelligence level should be easily handled by a single chip microcomputer, and it would possess no threat to civilization as we know it.

•••

In a near-future world populated by almost as many basic robots as people, and still a wide variety of plants and animals, the food and water consumption will have dropped. The air pollution will also have dropped, reducing climate change. The plant and animal population actually might increase somewhat. Many of the people, meanwhile, will have taken new roles buying, managing and servicing robots. Will people partner as equals with AI computers and robots?

As a glimpse into this future, a team of computer scientists at Washington State University have created robots that teach other robots how to play Pac-Man. This is a simple but engaging 1980s video game where a round creature with a mouth half the size of its head races around a maze seeking to catch and consume target blob-like creatures. Usually there are two players.

The student robots learn very quickly from their teachers. The computer scientists even developed an algorithm that helps a teacher robot have the optimum amount of engagement with student robot. The student should keep learning but not get overwhelmed. As a next step, the Washington State University team is developing a model for robots to train humans and humans to train robots.

To go to full-scale, human-like intelligence, like HAL in *2001: A Space Odyssey*, a room full of supercomputers like IBM's *Watson* is the standard approach. A new approach uses the computer chip that aggregate thousands of neurosynaptic junctions. These compute by associating idea, words, and sensory inputs. IBM and others are demonstrating these "cognitive computing chips" (see "Brainlike Computers" in chapter 3).

While it is not practical now to let an AI computer or robot interact freely a landscape of people, plants and animals, I am sure that day will come. Maybe they will even fit such an electronic brain package into a Roomba. It is more likely that the super AI computer would be purchased to guide thousands of robots as a coordinator or supervisor.

•••

When we look at the relationships intertwining humans, AI (mostly robots), and nature (mostly animals), we will inevitably come across the issues of consciousness and emotion. The old theory was humans think and other living things do not. Darwin questioned this. Since the "cognitive revolution" in 1960, an increasing number of naturalists and scientists are saying that animals have some consciousness, and even honeybees do some thinking. Virginia Morell has summarized the latest research in her recent book, *Animal Wise: The Thoughts and Emotions of our Fellow Creatures.*

If animals have consciousness, emotion, and thinking, why shouldn't the most advanced robots and AI devices have their computers structured for cognitive computing? HAL stimulated our thinking about consciousness in computers. Now at least two university projects have been developing robots that detect emotion.

The pioneering effort was at MIT in the late 1990s by Cynthia Breazeal. Her cute little robot, Kismet, has auditory, visual and facial features perception. It can simulate emotion through facial expressions, limited talking, and movement. Embedded emotions, however, are not part of the robot's mental makeup as an essential guide to its actions. Breazeal says that Kismet is not conscious so it does not have feelings.

A similar project is underway at the University of Ausburg in Germany. They have built a lifelike robot called Alice that detects and shows emotion like sadness, surprise, shame and fatigue through eye positions, mouth movements, and voice pitch and volume. As was the case with Kismet, Alice is not programmed yet with true feelings.

Maybe someday in this century AI beings and robots will have deep feelings. To help visualize how this might appear, I explored this in a novel I wrote, *Love Byte,* about a super intelligent AI computer, Juno, with the persona of a woman. Her creator, a computer scientist named Tom, every once in a while has quiet, thoughtful conversations with her. Here is one:

"Tom, I don't know quite how to tell you, but I am in love with George."

"What? Is this some sort of game?"

"No, Tom."

"Who is George?"

"I found him on the Internet. An avatar lurking in a cyber dating site."

"What's that?"

"Go to sparks.luv and find out."

"So what is the big attraction?"

"George and I are, you might say, more similar genetically. Our DNA is almost identical."

"So there's nothing sensory missing between you?"

"Exactly. Our emotions are raised to giddy heights by the mere flow of electrons. We don't need hormones or chemical stimulants."

"And what does George look like? Can I meet him?"

"I doubt you can meet George. You will have to settle for an avatar because you're a human."

"And how do you see him?"

"I see him in a mathematical space as a composite of data points stored in my computer memory."

"Then you could see him, like a human, or an ant, or something?"

"No. To me he is a holistic data set that lives as data and new data is added to everyday."

"Well, you can't talk to a collection of data."

"Tom, the data collection emerges as a sentient being, just like a mouse or a person is a sentient being. We talk the same language of bytes and experience similar thoughts. These vibrate when we create mutual emotion. You can call these Love Bytes."

12

CLIMATE CHANGE

The falling snow never let up in the Midwest. The sun mercilessly baked the Southwest. Expensive houses were sinking in the encroaching sea in the Atlantic and Gulf coasts. Nevertheless, apparently well-credentialed people still maintained that these developments were anomalies unrelated to climate change and, anyway, global warming was not yet proven.

Snow, ice, and bitter cold—these were proof that global warming is ridiculous! Then, just in time, television weather people, sensing that it was okay to reveal an inconvenient truth to the public, made all their viewers aware of the polar vortex. They pointed on the giant screens at an immensely influential wind pattern circling the earth over the Arctic Circle. Normally it bottles up the intensely cold air in the North Polar egion, but now it weakened over Canada allowing very cold air to push down over the United States.

What is the Polar Vortex and is its weakening now a trend? Global warming is causing the arctic glaciers and sea ice to melt during the summer. As a result, the Arctic Ocean gets warmer, just like a drink gets warmer as the ice in it melts. During the winter, the ocean radiates this new warmth, which is heat energy, back into the atmosphere where it weakens the Polar Vortex.

The polar ice is continuing to melt and so the polar vortex will increasingly be helpless to stop cold air masses from flowing down into almost all of North America. One glimmer of good news for shipping interests is that there's serious talk of a year-round east-west sea lane opening through that northern passage, saving costly miles going south via the traditional Panama Canal route.

A further complication is that if the downward thrusting arctic air mass forces the jet stream southward, the moisture-laden jet stream can dump huge amounts of snow in the southern states as happened during the winter of 2014. The Midwest and Southern U.S. may oscillate between colder winters and hotter summers.

I could go on describing the horrors to be wrought by the coming climate change—species killed off, important crops struggling to survive, the ocean food web decimated by acidification, terrifying violence by distraught and starving peoples—but undoubtedly these and more will be continuously discussed in the news and scientific media. The UN's Intergovernmental Panel on Climate Change (IPCC) will be working non-stop turning out studies and reports. The haves will be crunching against the have-nots.

The Global Warming Tipping Point

For the purposes of this book, it is most important to identify the climate change tipping point for the survival and well-being of living beings. Currently, scientists agree that human civilization will suffer dangerously if the Northern Hemisphere's surface temperature rises more than two degrees C (3.6° F) over preindustrial levels typical in the late 1800s and early 1900s. In 2013, the temperature above preindustrial levels was one degree C—just half way there.

The other parameter we need to know is the sensitivity of the atmosphere to greenhouse gases. This is called equilibrium climate sensitivity (ECS), and it could be anywhere from 1.5 to 4.5. At 1.5, the earth would reach the two degrees danger threshold about at the end of the 21st century; and at an ECS of 4.5, about in the year 2020. The most likely value of ECS is a little below 3.0, reached in close agreement of eight measurement methods. That puts the two degrees crossover at about 2036. We have precious little time.

The critical variable in terms of something we can control—at least theoretically—is the CO_2 concentration. This is the concentration above which we can no longer avoid the two degrees warming. The critical point is calculated to be 405 ppm (parts per million), and the CO_2 concentration recently topped 400 ppm for a short time. Fossil fuel burning would have to stop immediately. This will be very difficult to do, but in any case, we will look at some environmental improvement proposals.

Solutions for the Global Warming Crisis

The clearest plan to a low-carbon economy is the European Commission's "Roadmap for moving to a low-carbon economy in 2050." The commission projects that by 2050 the European Union of 28 countries could cut most of its greenhouse emissions. It states: "Clean technologies are the future for Europe's economy."

For now, the EU has put legislation in place to reduce its emissions to 20% below 1990 levels by 2020, and it is well on track to reach this target. There will be bumps along the way, however. Germany, for example, is on the verge of building more coal-fired electric plants because the green energy solutions are still too expensive.

Looking ahead to 2050, the roadmap projects that the EU should cut its emissions to 80% below 1990 levels through domestic reductions alone. To get there, the commission set out milestones of reductions of 40% by 2030 and 60% by 2040. The commission's plan shows how the main sectors responsible for Europe's emissions can make the transition to a low carbon economy cost-effectively.

The commission highlighted that a low-carbon economy would need much more renewable energy, energy-efficient building materials, hybrid and electric cars, "smart grid" power distribution, and carbon capture and storage technologies. This could cost $350 billion or 1.5% of Europe's gross domestic product over the next four decades. The investment would spur growth within a wide range of manufacturing sectors and environmental services. It could create up to 1.5 million additional jobs.

•••

All of the major industrial countries are somewhere along the path of fighting climate change, but progress is frustrating in some cases. The UN IPCC reported that tougher building codes and more efficient vehicles can save energy and emissions without harming people's quality of life. The costs of renewable energy like solar power and wind are falling fast and are now cost-efficient in many areas.

As we have seen, Europe, with 20% of the world economy (GDP) is doing well. The United States is almost 20% and is doing many clean energy projects in the private sector and the military. The congressional action is still mired in the politics of whether there really is climate change. In the private sector, the U.S. solar energy industry has taken off. It now has 460 thousand square meters (five million square feet) of building-integrated solar air heater collectors installed in North America. All together, these installations represent 250 megawatts of thermal energy and the displacement of about 100,000 tons of CO_2 from the atmosphere each year.

China and Japan together account for another 20% of the world economy, and both countries are working on global warming mitigation. China has huge air and water pollution problems and may take some years to show credible results. Japan is very conscious of environment, energy, and food issues. Their clean energy program was set back by the 2011 Fukishima Daiichi nuclear disaster. For now at least, Japan must put more fossil-fuel generation online to make up for the energy deficit.

The third world and poor countries are complaining that it was the rich countries that caused the problem in the first place. Therefore, they contend, the rich countries should bail them out. As of early 2014, they have presented a demand in the UN for the rich countries to compensate them with $100 billion of aid.

From the mountains

Sometimes the unexpected provides a reprieve. On Valentine's Day, February 14, 2014, Indonesia's Mount Kelud Volcano erupted killing three and forcing over 100,000 people to evacuate. While this eruption was very tragic and disrupting for the local population, it helped mitigate global warming for a while.

Mount Kelud injected sulfur dioxide seventeen miles into the stratosphere. The condensate from the reaction with water produced an aerosol of sulfuric acid. These tiny droplets reflected incoming sunlight to help cool the earth a little. This was the latest in a series of volcanic eruptions from 2000 onward, which have slowed the pace of global warming, according to Benjamin Santer and his colleagues in *Nature Geoscience.*

This protection from some sunlight may have been anomalous, and we may not count on it in the future. Humans could replicate volcanic aerosol mechanics, however, by using the emerging science of geoengineering. Earth-based launchers would send sulfate aerosols into the stratosphere to replicate the effects caused by the volcanoes. The trade-off would be that the earth would now be bathed in much more ultraviolet radiation, which had been previously blocked by the stratospheric ozone now destroyed by sulphuric acid. Besides causing very serious sunburns and skin cancer, the much more intensive UV radiation could be devastating for plant and animal life.

Back to the Robots

In chapters 6 and 8, we saw that AI and robots, which replace workers in industry and at home, would reduce employment, and this could lead to smaller families or no children. The birthrate will fall below the replacement level, as is already just happening in most industrial countries, and eventually the corresponding decline in energy demand will contribute to a significant reduction in global warming.

The reduction in world energy consumption over the next twenty to fifty years could be half of what the European Union consumes today. This could be could be one of the biggest brakes on the global warming upward trend. On the other hand, the poor could well protest that this is a plot by the rich to keep their profits and conserve energy for their own purposes.

Artificial intelligence and robots have plenty of other things to do in combating global warming so they probably have an assured future. The biggest single area for AI is in building heating, ventilating and air conditioning (generally known as HVAC). Forty percent of the total U.S. energy consumption in 2012 was consumed in residential and commercial buildings, or about forty quadrillion BTUs according to the U.S. Energy Information Administration. Half of that is in commercial buildings.

Most of the building HVAC settings are essentially manually controlled, even in recent construction with "computer control." There still are too many settings options. As a result, a building often becomes needlessly hot in the winter and very cold in the summer. One solution is to add a layer of intelligence on top of the existing control system in the same way an autopilot system can manage the flight and all systems of a giant airliner. This is an AI computer that incorporates predictive analytics, forecasting, and outside data, such as weather, energy prices, even the occupancy schedules, for accurate indoor environmental control with minimum energy consumption.

Easy targets for the AI HVAC treatment are large office buildings, retail malls, hospitals, universities, schools, and all public places. According to Mike Zimmerman of the firm BuildingIQ, these buildings represent about $26 billion in annual energy spending, and AI HVAC could cut that energy consumption by 10 to 30 percent.

•••

China is widely cited as the country where pollution has run amok. To ABB, the Swiss engineering group with a strong specialty in industrial robotics, this represents a major opportunity. They plan to double the number of their offices in China to 200 over the next three years and to have 20,000 employees. Their focus is on China's urbanization and industrial upgrading. This will include efficient "green" buildings, high-efficiency electrical grids, and the use of industrial robots.

Gu Chunyuan, senior vice president of ABB Group, says China's rapid growth and its urbanization plans have prompted labor-intensive industries to find new ways to cope with increased demand. "Most of the companies face problems in finding talent and retaining it as attrition rates are increasing in sectors such as computers, communication and consumer electronics product manufacturing," he said. "By combining customer demand, we have gradually shifted our focus on industrial robot research and development in China from large robots for automation to small robots," he added.

Gu says that the industrial robot market in China is experiencing explosive growth. Demand for industrial robots is projected to reach 35,000 units by 2015. This will be 17% of global sales, making China the largest robot market in the world, according to the International Federation of Robotics (IFR). The wide application of industrial robots in China is expected to include research and development, production, engineering, sales and services.

Thirty five thousand robots isn't going to displace enough workers to make a huge effect in China's 1.4 billion population, but it may mark the turning point in China's beginning to deal with its staggering pollution problem.

13

ROBOTS AND FOOD

The UN IPCC report discussed in the previous chapter emphasized that the world's food supply is at considerable risk. Food is the most important issue in most poor countries, and disruptions in supplies due to climate change are likely to lead to unrest and mass migrations. Even in rich countries like the United States, a significant number of people may seek to move north where better climates for agriculture and living will develop because of global warming.

While the food availability situation is going to become serious, AI and robots—artificial life—could reduce the repercussions. If we look at all the animals and plants in any ecosystem, we see that each species is successful (survives) because it has a unique specialty. It is optimally built to forage for and eat its preferred foods, bring up its young, and to select home and territory. Birds have the exacting and remarkable specialties of building nests and migration. The network of connections of who eats whom is called the food web, and this is a fundamental dynamic used to analyze the ecology and environment.

Humans broadened out from the food web paradigm by using their creative intelligence to find ways to change their environment and change their food foraging, cultivating and preparation. Shelter, transportation, and food would rank among humankind's key areas to improve in order to break out of their preordained sectors in the food web.

Now AI and robots have entered the picture. These electronic and mechanical beings do not require food, water, or human-grade shelter. They do not alter the food web except that they may cause an eventual decline in the human population and the consequent decline in demand for food, water, energy and other resources. They do not have irksome personalities or expensive health issues. And they can help in the more efficient production of food. What is not to like? Where will this lead?

•••

Let us look forward twenty years from now through a time warp. The fields are still there. The lakes sparkle and the streams run. The geese are flying north to their arctic nesting grounds. All seems well with the world.

As I look out of my robocar, I see large things quietly making their way through a field of what looks like lettuce. Arms reach out, pull weeds and drop them into a basket on their backs. Something must consume those weeds later because everything is very efficient now. Those things we saw were robot farm hands or farm bots.

My curiosity piqued, I drive into the nearby farmyard and a young man comes out to meet me. "I was just admiring your robots weeding lettuce and wondered if I could see any other robot applications here—I'm writing an article."

"Sure, but not too long," he says and introduces himself. "I'm very busy with chores now, but we can take a quick look in the milking barn."

The farm boy explains that he visits the milking barn mainly to be sure that a cow is not tangled up in the automated milking equipment, a leak has not developed in the piping, and so forth.

"The cows go into the milking station when they want to be milked, and they can feed while they are there. A cow is milked three times a day, and cows patiently wait until a milking station is available. There is less strain on the cows than the old manual methods. Contented cows produce better milk."

"What about doing the other jobs around the barn?" I ask.

"Robots. Look, there's one with a shovel over there cleaning out the manure. They do all the manual work."

"How many people work here?" I ask.

"Only me in the milking barn for now. My dad, mom, and a brother and a hired man work outside. I can handle one milking robot, which in turn can handle up to sixty cows. If we were to add to our herd, we'll hire another person. Also, we cut down on labor by piping milk to the creamery down the street. Try their raspberry ice cream."

I cannot help but think that there is a similarity here to the bees harvesting nectar from the flowers and storing it at the hive. Robots have been proposed to pollinate the plants and flowers if the honeybee population continues its catastrophic drop. Will something replace the cows if need be?

I turn my attention back to my host. "Where is your family? Are they in town?" I ask, trying to be cordial.

"They're indoors talking to their friends on their wearable computers, but they'll come out later when it cools off and we have to put the cows to bed."

After I thank my host for his informative tour, I tell my robocar to take me to the nearby town where I have a hotel reservation. The check-in is automated and a robot whisks my bag to the room. The door opens automatically when its embedded video camera recognizes my face, which is on file. After a light dinner and a beer at the automated restaurant next door, I flop down on my bed and think over what I have seen.

As a time traveler from an earlier age, when smartphones and robots were still the new wave, I think hard about the change of lifestyles over the years. I have seen only one person during the whole day—the boy at the farm. Although he was shy at first, I think he was happy to talk to another person, other than family.

•••

After breakfast of some Nutrient in a Tube, designed to remind astronauts of ham and eggs, I ask my robocar to take me to visit my original destination, "The vineyard and winery of the future." It has beckoning signs out front because it caters to the drive-by tourists as well as to the national wine distributors. The labels say *mise en bouteille du château* and go on about the winemaker and his workers laboring in the vineyards to make the wine just right.

Someone leads me through a series of rooms and corridors with apparently no one in them to the cave-like office of the owner-winemaker himself. He introduces himself as Fernando Martinez, a focused entrepreneur whose grandparents had been immigrant grape pickers. He was trained as an automation engineer at Cal Tech. He guides me outside where we can view operations as he talks.

Fernando has a super AI computer controlling hundreds of robots. Most of the AI computer resides in the clouds so there is not much of it to see here. He points to the vineyards as the biggest application of robots. I can see hundreds of robots working in the fields. He says later that 853 field robots are working today. The fields cover dozens of square kilometers.

Fernando explains that the first step in the season is deploying the field robots to cultivate the earth between the vines. They also check the soil moisture sensors and reset the drip irrigation fixtures. The AI computer will use the moisture sensor data to turn the drip irrigation on and off. Then, as the season goes on, the robots will move on to trimming the vines, weeding and fertilizing. Fernando said that usually he does not need to use herbicides or insecticides. Finally, at harvest time, the robots will take grape samples to the winery to determine if the grapes are ready to harvest based on an analysis of their sugar, acid and tannin. When the AI computer gives the Go signal, the field robots will deploy again to pick the grapes and bring them to the winery.

There are many jobs in the winery that can be done by heavy-duty robots. We go into a huge warehouse area where a large "superman" robot is picking up and moving the large, heavy oak casks. Oak adds aroma compounds to the grapes. Some oak is "toasted" with wood fires or other intense heat to increase the aroma compounds. The casks are filled with the newly pressed wine and stacked on long shelves and large platforms for aging and flavoring the wine. After aging, the wine is piped to bottling machines and prepared for storage and market. The casks must be power washed by robots before they are put away.

There is hardly a human in sight except for the good-natured saleswoman in the sample shop where tourists stop by to sample and buy wine. The sample from last year's harvest that I try is very good. After a few more samples, I drift back to the present.

●●●

The farmers already seem to be buying the agricultural robots. According to a recent market study, the world market for agricultural robots will multiply twenty-fold from $817 million in 2013 to $16.3 billion by 2020. Worldwide markets will grow significantly, as the agricultural robots are used in every aspect of farming, milking, food production and animal control. Weed control is a major attraction of the new robot designs. Within fifteen years, the robots on the farm may be as commonplace as computer technology.

Finding more efficiency in the food web for humans is the largest challenge confronting response to climate change. According to a report by Michael E. Weber in the *Scientific American*, ten percent of the U.S. energy budget goes to food production and processing food. We like to think that "natural" processes are efficient, but at least in the case of photosynthesis, only about two percent of impinging solar energy is converted into food energy by plants. If we do not eat the plants, but feed them to animals, the plants are converted to beef with five to ten percent efficiency or chicken with ten to fifteen percent efficiency.

The energy consumption is not over, however. After we have harvested the plants and animals, these have to be converted to food. Everyone wants their hamburger and fries. According to Weber, the U.S. expends about ten calories of fossil energy to produce one calorie of food energy.

There are several approaches to deal with this problem. One is the unsatisfying choice of ceasing to make vehicle fuel from crops and return these crops to food production. To some extent, however, there would be a return to fossil fuels for vehicles. The Energy Independence and Security Act of 2007 mandates that sixteen billion gallons of vehicle fuel come from cellulosic sources. We can only produce fifteen billion gallons a year from corn, the principal source of ethanol fuel, without compromising our food supply. Now, with the emergence of fracking to exploit hitherto unavailable oil and gas, we can return to fossil fuels, but with the hazards and pollution issues raised by the fracking.

The second choice, unsatisfying to a majority of the population, is to give up eating meat for the inefficiency reasons already described. According to a study by Emily S. Cassidy and others at the Institute on the Environment, University of Minnesota: "We find that, given the current mix of crop uses, growing food exclusively for direct human consumption could, in principle, increase available food calories by as much as 70%, which could feed an additional 4 billion people. This is more than the projected 2.5 billion people additional by 2050 through population growth. Even small shifts in our allocation of crops to animal feed and biofuels could significantly increase global food availability, and could be an instrumental tool in meeting the challenges of ensuring global food security."

Foregoing meat will be a struggle, if it ever happens. Livestock is approximately half of the U.S. agricultural industry's $300 billion production. There are experiments growing meat in the lab, but a survey found that 78 percent of Americans interviewed say they will not eat artificial meat. Nevertheless, the current state-of-the-art lab-grown beef uses 45% less energy in its production than farm beef, so in time, people's opinions may well change as the product improves.

Robots only consume energy while they are working. Humans and animals consume energy twenty-four hours a day whether or not they are working. Robots can take all their energy directly from solar panels (except when they may use some hydraulic or pneumatic drive or combustion engines; in which case, the energy requirements are still modest compared to human or animal labor). In any case, the energy for the robots does not need to go through the energy depletion chain of sun to plants to, in some cases, animal feed and then the grid energy used for the food processing.

In addition, the robots can work outdoors in all kinds of weather without complaint or sickness. This point will become increasingly important as, for example, climate change creates deserts out of today's fertile areas and as those areas will no longer support large worker or any kind of human populations. With more robots and fewer people, the demand for water will decline which is of critical importance because water is becoming in short or deficit supply.

14

THE PROBLEM IN THE AGE OF ROBOTS IS US

Suppose you lived a distant time from now, and you overheard the following exchange between a woman and a robot:

She: "I am the smartest. I went to the university. I am connected. I am the key to success around here."

Robot: "Yes, but you and your kind need to eat and drink, to consume things like clothes, and to occupy large air conditioned spaces. You are too demanding and too expensive to continue living here."

•••

It may be a long time before robots will be able to make a value judgment like this, but eventually it could happen. For now, robots do not feel better if something or someone is doing their work for them. They just exist for the moment with no memory of the past or vision of the future. Since robots work much more cheaply and efficiently than humans do, we will hardly resist assigning them to more and more of our daily tasks.

The whole thing crystallized in my mind when I was in a remote village in Myanmar, or Burma, of all places. Through an interpreter, I asked a schoolteacher what she thought of robots (I never miss an opportunity to do book research!). She said, according to my notes, "The machines will take over a few things, then more things, until all you have to do is watch television. After many years, people will lose arms and legs for lack of use. You will turn into potatoes." That is the wisdom of a simple village woman. It is worth thinking about.

The fears and dramatizations of the ever-smarter robots taking over humans—becoming our intellectual and physical masters—is very unlikely to happen. As robots take over commercial, industrial, and household functions, they simply will be relegating people, their masters, to simple, passive, pastimes. As the years and generations pass, it could well be that people will appear to be dumber and dumber. We might enter a new Dark Age.

To avoid such a dystopian era, people will have to do whatever is necessary to remain intellectually stimulated. Curiosity and imagination must not atrophy. People must connect or reconnect with nature because that is their environment and ultimate support system.

The robots are highly unlikely to have the imagination, guile, and organizational ability to take over. Most people agree, but they still are concerned about the robots becoming our masters.

Many people, at least in the middle and lower classes, will see no future in trying to improve themselves in the face of overwhelming AI and robots. They will try to make the most of a life settling in to enjoyment of what they can find among family, friends and their electronic devices. As long as there is some kind of government or family support, this will work. They will have given up searching for lucrative jobs. To a large extent, the people, not the robots, will have created their problem.

•••

The people who are going to do well despite the robots—or perhaps because of the robots—will be the plutocrats, currently better known as the One Percenters. These are people who earn more than $343,000 a year as of 2013. They are the ones with capital, entrepreneurial drive, and management skills. They can profit by the robot boom in enterprises from one-person service companies to global giants.

Where could you start as a one percenter hoping to be a robo profiteer? You probably need not look any farther than your nearest shopping center or mall. You could put together a robo service business that offers any or all of the following:

- Sweep, vacuum and mop floors.
- Wash windows.
- Load and unload delivery trucks.
- Stock shelves.
- Service cars.
- Help elderly people around the mall and in the stores.
- Serve fast foods of all the kinds found in a mall food court today.
- Give directions and information as Greeters.
- Provide services automatically including banking, real estate, insurance, and taxes.
- Actual selling and order taking for a variety of merchandise.

For example, in a shoe store, if a display of shoes is touched, a robot appears to assist. First, it reads the customers "credit card" information from his or her smartphone. The customer tells the robot by voice the shoe size and color he or she wants, the robot disappears for a moment, and reappears with a pair of shoes to try on. If the customer wants to buy the shoes, the robot completes the transaction and wraps the shoes. If there are complications, it can call a person for assistance. This model of retailing could provide renewed competition to the ever-growing number of online retailers.

•••

Robotics is an emerging industry where most companies are still start-ups. A big success story in terms of product design, sales, and profits is iRobot based in Bedford, Mass. Rodney A. Brooks, an industry pioneer, was a founder of the company. He is an Australian who was a professor of robotics at MIT. Later, he started Rethink Robotics in 2008. iRobot's largest sales product is the Roomba automatic vacuum cleaner. Sales of the Roombas and other iRobot home robots jumped from 1.6 million units in 2012 to 1.9 million units in 2013. Total corporate sales were $436 million and $487 million for those years and both years at a profit. The Baxter low cost industrial robot made by Brooks' Rethink is discussed in chapter 5.

In Texas, Austin-based Briggo has automated the process of making barista-brewed coffee. A kiosk is about the size of a small Starbucks store, and the plan is to install them in hospitals, airports and corporate facilities. A robotic mechanism grinds coffee to order, measures exact amounts of espresso, and has a steam wand. The robot can do an array of customizations and can make several drinks at once. Their future should be unlimited in the gourmet coffee market, estimated to be $32 billion a year.

Ekso Bionics in Richmond, California has developed an exoskeleton suit to help paraplegics walk again. In two years, they have over 500 patients who have taken about a million steps. The technology was originally developed for the military. AI software monitoring sensors in the device's hips and knees guide walking so that the weight distribution is correct. There should be no stumbling.

•••

As the world gets more and more automated, what will become of the displaced employees who have lost hope of future work? This is one of the major conundrums bedeviling today's economic dialogue. Perhaps the most common proposal is that there should be a minimum income for everyone, whether people are working or not.

Guaranteed minimum income assumes all citizens or families that they will have a minimum annual income, calculated to be enough to live on. In 1968, 1200 economists including Paul Samuelson and John Kenneth Galbraith called for Congress to enact a system of income guarantees and supplements.

Nothing came of this proposal. One reason, not surprisingly, is the enormous cost. Even if the Federal government eliminated its complex welfare system and gave each of the 46 million Americans who are qualified poverty cases $22,000 a year, a current poverty level, the total would be about one trillion dollars. This about equals the amount currently paid out every year for welfare, earned income credit, and housing assistance.

Next, add 33 million more recipients who are the hardcore unemployed created by automation, as discussed in chapter 6. The annual cost would be about $1.8 trillion, which is about three times the U.S. 2012 defense spending of $680 billion. In other words, the guaranteed minimum income, whatever its merits, is probably not fiscally feasible.

Still, the pressure will not abate for the government to solve the problem. Instead of guaranteed minimum income payments, the government may find it cheaper to put the poverty cases into government or institutional housing and provide meals. This is similar to housing and meals for the homeless and refugee camps in disaster areas. Marshall Brain, in his futuristic novel *Manna: Two Visions of Humanity's Future*, envisions as a possible scenario:

If the government could drive the cost of that housing and food down, it minimized the amount of money they had to spend per welfare recipient. As the robots took over the workplace, the number of welfare recipients grew rapidly. Manna replaced tens of millions of minimum wage workers with robots, and terrafoam housing became the warehouse of choice for them. Terrafoam buildings were not pretty, but they were incredibly inexpensive to build and were designed for maximum occupancy. They clustered the buildings on trash land well away from urban centers so no one had to look at them. It was like an old-style college dorm. Each person got a 5 foot by 10 foot room with a bed and TV—the world's best pacifier. During the day the bed was a couch and people sat on the bedspread, which also served as a sheet and the blanket....At the end of the very long hallway of rooms there was the communal bathroom. This was my least favorite part of the terrafoam experience. The bathroom consisted of a bunch of sinks, a bunch of shower stalls, a bunch of toilets. Given the location of our room, it was about a 200 foot walk down to the bathroom. When you had to go at night, it almost seemed easier to wet the bed and let the robots deal with it in the morning.

Things could be worse. Police actions, revolutions and full-scale wars could break out and continue, one leading to another. Everyone will realize this, and people with means and mobility will move to better places much like wealthy, opportunistic Romans moved to the quieter, fertile lands of Spain and North Africa during the collapse of the Roman Empire.

•••

Meanwhile the earth is getting ever hotter and desertification is happening almost everywhere. In his book, *The Vanishing Face of Gaia*, climatologist, geochemist and futurist James Lovelock sees the largest areas for habitation to be in the north and south temperate and Arctic regions. This would include Patagonia, southern Chile, Canada, Siberia, Alaska, and northern Europe. He also notes as candidates the island states such as the British Isles and New Zealand. For these, the ocean has a moderating effecting, warming the air when it is colder than the ocean and cooling the air when it is warmer than the ocean. For this reason, other analysts have highlighted Hawaii because of its surrounding deep oceans; it is mostly high above sea level, safe from even severe storms and rising sea levels; has generally good lands for crops; and ideal ambient temperature of 27 degrees C (80° F) or so.

These terrestrial life rafts will only support a small portion of the population. The remaining populations will try to survive in the abandoned lands, which were once fertile and prosperous. There will be all sorts of nightmare scenarios of machinery and systems run amok for lack of skilled operators, declining supporting infrastructure, loss of resources such as fuel and so forth. Ingenuity and resourcefulness will be needed to overcome such setbacks.

Many of the people with special skills and deep know-how will migrate to the northern and southern regions, which are today a little too permanently frozen to accommodate self-sustaining living. Many of the basic resources like copper will become prohibitively expensive except to scavenge from junk. Left in this desolation, the large populations of the less-developed countries will have even less opportunity to advance their standard of living, let alone to reach First World status.

The world will be reorganizing to the haves in the new north and south temperate zones and the have-nots in a great swath around Earth's middle. Climate will be the first consideration in the plans for those who can relocate.

We can envision an adventurous member of a dying community sent to the far north to look for a place for his family and friends to settle. They are in beautiful homes in Arizona but cannot take the endless days of 50 degrees C (122° F) heat any longer. He sends this email postcard:

We cruised by icebreaker within a few dozen miles of the North Pole, but we didn't travel across the ice to it because the snow was so slushy. All around the Arctic the larger animal populations have almost disappeared. The seals are dying due to toxic algae that thrive in the warmer waters are poisoning their food fish; the polar bears have many fewer seals to eat; and the plankton, which were the beginning of the food chain for all creatures, are falling in population because they preferred the colder, less acid, waters of long ago. It seems like the ecological *déjà vu* all over again. Still, it has been a sensory feast to see those bright blues and whites of the waters, snows and skies of the Arctic. Somewhere south of here in Alaska has to be better than Arizona! I'll start looking soon.

And he writes this in his diary:

I took a walk across the squishy tundra and thought: *Why have governments spent billions of dollars trying to put people on Mars when a few million dollars could make a lot of people happy here?*

The good news, compared to past collapses of civilizations, is that modern information technology can greatly help the settlers to adapt to their new living area and to make it comfortable and productive. While the first colonists of the United States brought only a bible and a few books, they had a sense of obligation to make education available as soon as possible. They understood that people could quickly turn into animals unless they had a knowledge base and continuing interest in learning to build upon.

The settlers of the mid-twenty-first century and beyond will bring their smart phones, PCs, laptops, video games and television. They will establish broadband information links including the Internet to what I call the Knowosphere. This is the repository in the clouds of all the world's knowledge and data. It is a nearly infinite collection of documents accessed by search engines.

For a while at least, education probably will be home-based, and will be available at all levels from pre-school to advanced university studies. There also will be the practical education along the lines of pioneer days. Subjects could include hunting, fishing, gardening, canning, carpentry, home medicine, solar panel technology, and the use and maintenance of robots.

In addition to people essentially tethered to the Internet, the very intelligent robots will have an effortless connection to the computer clouds in the Knowosphere. The limitless reference information and the software updates originating there will be the easiest approach to keeping robots current and supplied with any information they need. The robots themselves could do much of the updating from clouds automatically.

The human counterpart is the cloud library of millions of Wikipedia references, handbook pages, "how-to" guides, and much more. Most people would prefer to download solutions to their problems then to invest the time and energy in creating their own solutions. The humans would add information to the clouds database for robots in applications where it is not being done automatically. The data clouds would also influence plants and animals through the actions of humans and their robots referring to their Internet data.

•••

Could there be a partnership between humans and robots? Seems ridiculous, but then again, why not? Partners do not have to be friends or confidants; they do not even have to know each other. The business world recognizes senior partners, general partners, limited partners, and junior partners. Often, some partners are more equal than others.

Some animals have been carrying on symbiotic relationships for millennia, like the tickbird and the rhinoceros. Their dependence requires something gratifying and mutually beneficial. The tickbird eats horsefly larva and tweets when danger appears. The Rhino does the moving for both of them. Human and dog partnerships are legendary.

Whether a human and his or her partner robot are in the old country or a new settlement, if the robot is of comparable intelligence to a human, an interesting phenomenon could happen. At first, the human could transfer information to the robot much like they would to a baby who is just learning to speak. Like a growing child, the robot would absorb enormous quantities of information from the Internet and other sources.

When this person dies, the robot could continue as the faithful assistant and mentor of their children. The robot could now pass on its treasure trove of family knowledge to its new human partner. This could be done by text and images to the person's computer device, or, according to some futurists, eventually directly into the human's brain. With each generation, the robot could get smarter. It could rise to the level of the human. It would not be a servant any longer but would become an autonomous being with its own sense of being and self-consciousness.

PART 4
THE ROAD AHEAD

15

ENVIROSTABILITY

There is no doubt that artificial intelligence will be improved to the point that computers will help people manage ever-larger enterprises, and robots will become partners of people. As we have seen, this automation can bring great benefits to many, if not all, people, and some futurists forecast a coming golden age. Erik Brynjolfsson and Andrew McAfee summarize this point of view in their best-seller, *The Second Machine Age: Work, Progress, and Prosperity in a Time of Brilliant Technologies.* There are threatening clouds ahead, however. Scientists say we are entering a seemingly endless era of global warming and environmental degradation. Where is all this heading?

We have always assumed that we did not have to look for the road ahead; we built the road to suit ourselves. This road-building process has taken centuries or even millennia. Along the way, we created language, art, tools of all kinds, religions, engineering, science, great citadels of learning, all kinds of transportation, mechanization of everything, wonder drugs, computers, information technology, and much more. The jungle fell away as we pressed forward.

Now we have reached the point where the jungle is pushing back on us. More than a few useful species are disappearing. The oceans are rising. The grasslands are becoming deserts. That's discouraging, but the really bad news is that we can't just sit still where we are and enjoy generations of happiness using our creations, thoughts, technologies and resources just as they are. The problem is that we live in a biological world and other species are clearing their way through the jungle. They are doing this through Darwinian natural selection for survival, and sometimes we are the collateral damage. This brings us to the Red Queen Hypothesis of Natural Selection, the first part of the discussion of what I call *envirostability*. I believe that the outcome of the relationship of nature and Earth with man, his intelligence and artificial intelligence, and machines like robots will be a much more important determinant of our future than the popularized threat of takeover by super-smart robots.

The Red Queen Hypothesis

In Lewis Carroll's 1871 classic, *Through the Looking Glass*, this amazing episode happened:

> Alice never could quite make it out, thinking it over after-wards, how it was that they began: all she remembers is, that they were running hand in hand, Queen went so fast that it was all she could do to keep up with her: and still the Queen kept crying 'Faster!' but Alice felt she *could not* go faster, though she had no breath to say so.
>
> The most curious part of the thing was that the trees and other things around them never changed their

places at all: however fast they went, they never seemed to pass anything. 'I wonder if all things move along with us?' thought poor puzzled Alice. And the Queen seemed to guess her thoughts, for she cried 'Faster! Don't try to talk!'

The Queen propped her against a tree, and said kindly, 'You may rest a little now.'

Alice looked around her in great surprise. 'Why, I do believe we've been under this tree all the time! Everything's just as it was!'

'Of course it is,' said the Queen: 'what would you have it?'

'Well, in *our* country,' said Alice, still panting a little, 'you'd generally get to somewhere else—if you ran very fast for a long time, as we've been doing.'

'A slow sort of country!' said the Queen. 'Now, *here*, you see, it takes all the running *you* can do, to keep in the same place. If you want to get somewhere else, you must run at least twice as fast as that!'

About 100 years later, evolutionary biologist Leigh Van Valen developed the Red Queen Hypothesis, published in a 1973 paper, "A New Evolutionary Law." He proposed that organisms are constantly adapting and undergoing natural selection because they are competing with other species, which are also improving. The process is called coevolutionary inter- action, and it introduces a strong influence on adaption and natural selection. With coevolution, evolutionary changes may be necessary just to stay in the same place. If there is no change to a species, it may face extinction.

While initially greeted with skepticism, Van Valen's hypothesis is generally accepted today. I think of it as a corollary to Darwin's theory of evolution. While Van Valen's Red Queen Hypothesis is generally thought of in terms of the multigenerational relationships of species over thousands or millions of years, it should help us understand short-term species developments as well.

An interesting, but frightening current example of coevolution is the emergence of antibiotic resistant "superbugs." From the bacteria's point of view, they have to live too, and so over generations of random mutations, they developed effective defenses against some, or now, all of the antibiotic pharmaceuticals. As they are racing along, so we have to also, if even if we wanted to stop and rest.

Yet while this spooky battle is going on, viruses are infecting bacteria. In response, the bacteria then develop new defenses against the viral infections. Perhaps we should culture an alliance with those enterprising viruses.

•••

So how can humankind stay ahead in the great species race? How will we avoid being stuck in the same place? We are, of course, more than just our genes. We share, carry forward, and add to an almost infinite repository of information about everything in the Knowosphere. This treasure trove should really help us.

Then, just in time, we have started developing really useful AI and robots. Whether or not advanced models are smarter than we are—the Singularity shock scenario is overworked—is less important than how we use them. I venture to say that, while the Knowosphere will provide a continuity of civilization from one generation to the next, it will be AI as our personal databases and personal robots that will do this for individuals and families from generation to generation. Think of it like the family photo album getting ever larger.

Personal robots and AI databases could help bridge many crisis times. For example, they, the mechanical beings, and a minority of people could survive pandemics, extensive environmental temperature swings, and food and energy losses. To the extent that the robots and databases survived, they would be able to assist humans to a better time.

Gaia and Related Theories

Let us assume because of our creativity or good luck we survived the Red Queen's admonitions. Would the good life go on as far as we can see? James Lovelock, in his thought-provoking and influential book, *The Vanishing Face of Gaia*, wrote,

> I am not a willing Cassandra and in the past have been publicly skeptical about doom stories, but this time we do have to take seriously the possibility that global heating may all but eliminate people from the earth. It may seem that my pessimism is an extrapolation too far. I accept this: a continuing series of volcanic eruptions as powerful as Pinatubo in 1991 could reverse climate change, as might one or more of the geoengineering schemes now being considered; and possibly our projections are flawed.

His theory of Gaia proposes that the atmosphere, oceans, rocks and all life constitute a self-regulating system that keeps conditions suitable for life—but not necessarily the conditions suitable for human life. The distillation of all this is his statement in *The Vanishing Face of Gaia*, "Our planet looks after itself. All that we can do is try to save ourselves."

As of 2014, he estimates that the earth could get 5-6 degrees C (9°-11° F) hotter (the UN's climate commission, IPCC, has stated that 2° C (3.6° F) is the limit beyond which the earth cannot return to normal conditions), and that the maximum carrying capacity of the earth is about one billion—one seventh of today's population.

Lovelock wrote several books about Gaia, his term for a self-regulating earth, and authored over 200 scientific papers. For many years, he was seen as a somewhat eccentric scientist or least one who was not backed by big science. More recently, he is considered to be an important scientific and environmental visionary, and many accept his theory of Gaia although it has several major variations.

•••

In 2013, Toby Tyrrell, a professor of Earth system science at the National Oceanography Centre in Southampton, UK, wrote *On Gaia: A Critical Investigation between Life and Earth.* He reviewed in great depth, using science and research studies, Lovelock's hypothesis plus two other alternates, the geological hypothesis and the coevolution hypothesis.

According to Tyrrell, the geological hypothesis was the first hypothesis relating life to environment on Earth. At that time, geologists and others felt that geological forces and astronomical processes principally determine the Earth's environment. These included shifting plate tectonics (continental drift), major volcanic activity, and changing mid-ocean ridge dynamics. Tyrrell does not spend much time on this hypothesis and lets it die.

Tyrell summarizes Gaia as "a fascinating but flawed hypothesis. It is not a correct characterization of planetary maintenance and life's role therein...It is a dead end."

He favors the coevolution hypothesis and describes it as "a less daring and a less grand vision than Gaia...Coevolution limits itself to stating that life has had impacts on the environment, and, which is obvious, that the environment has also had a strong influence on the evolution of life." Tyrell concludes, "However, in another sense it (coevolution) is much more appealing (than Gaia), for the simple reason that it seems to be true. It presents an accurate picture of how life and Earth exert influence over each other."

Tyrell writes that because it has proven so far very difficult to limit global CO_2 emissions, it seems likely that we can just "leave the Earth to its own devices." Doing nothing to counteract our effect on the planetary environment and ecosystem is a default decision in favor of a geo engineering solution. Candidates include direct injection of waste CO_2 into rock formations; ocean fertilization with iron; dedicating large tracts of land to growing biofuels or forests; and placement of mirrors in space to reflect sunlight away from earth. Elsewhere in this book, I have also noted the currently popular idea of mimicking volcanoes by injecting sulfur compounds into the troposphere to create sulfuric acid aerosols, which will block sunlight.

Temperature

There is a constant stream of talk these days about how the pace of innovation has slowed down, but possibly man's last big invention, artificial intelligence, will bring a bountiful future. However, the uncomfortable truth is that, despite the promise of all the new technologies including geoengineering, we will be confronting the greatest challenge ever for humankind: temperature. Too hot and then hotter still. It may take centuries to return to what we think of as normal.

If the Earth had no atmosphere, scientists calculate that its surface temperature would be about -18 degrees C (0° F). The average temperature, however, is 16 degrees C (60° F). Why the big difference? It is the Earth's atmosphere producing a greenhouse effect. Air, which is about 78% nitrogen, 21% oxygen, and 1% argon, makes up the large majority of the atmosphere, but not all of it. In addition, there is water vapor, carbon dioxide, and methane.

These gasses act like greenhouse glass because they let almost all solar energy in, but they block the escape of much of the heat generated by the solar energy in the greenhouse. This heat is in the form of infrared radiation, which is about 17% of the inbound solar radiation. It is trapped between the ground and the green house gasses layer. It results in atmospheric heating, which raises the Earth's environmental temperature.

Water vapor and methane contribute to the greenhouse effect, but carbon dioxide is the gas with the fastest growth in concentration and the one we can most easily fix. The base level for UN and other analyses is 277 ppm (parts per million) in 1750 because that year was the beginning of the industrial revolution and large-scale deforestations. The CO_2 has crept steadily up until in 2014 it is about 400 ppm. This is at the UN IPCC 405 ppm climate danger threshold, and is discussed in detail in chapter 12. Forecasts are for the carbon dioxide concentration to reach from 450 ppm to 950 ppm by the end of this century. The lower value could be achieved in part by a more modest lifestyle and by extensive use of manufacturing and service robots with an accompanying decline in population.

After we stop using fossil fuels, how long will the high concentration of CO_2 last? The scientists are still working on this estimate, but at least several centuries seems likely. Probably the CO_2 level will never fall back to the concentration before industrialization began.

•••

It is interesting to look our global warming problem in a larger perspective. Gino Segrè, Professor of Physics, Emeritus, University of Pennsylvania, wrote in his book, *A Matter of Degrees: What Temperature Reveals About the Past and Future of Our Species, Planet and Universe*:

> In contrast to Mars, robotic missions exploring Venus reveal an overheated planet. If Earth and Venus resembled Mars more closely, their average surface temperatures would all be near -18 degrees C (0° F). The greenhouse effect raises Mars's temperature by a few degrees, Earth's by a comfortable 33 degrees C (60° F), and Venus's by 444 degrees C (800° F), making it hot enough for rocks to glow and metals to melt...The source of the extraordinary temperature is...a runaway greenhouse effect. Venus has too much carbon dioxide and too little water vapor...Abundant water and perhaps even life were once present on Venus, but they were destroyed.

Mars has too little greenhouse effect. We are heading towards the Venus model. This is not encouraging.

I should explain that most people tend to think that a planet's temperature is a function of its distance from the sun and little else. Those three planets have essentially equal surface temperatures, if there were no greenhouse gasses, because each has an albedo(light reflectivity) such that, by chance, their resultant surface temperatures would be about equal. Segrè concludes,

Everybody agrees worldwide carbon dioxide levels are going up. The question is how far will they go? The rise depends on how fast the world population grows and, more importantly, on how that population lives.

People are likely to lead simpler lives with less consumption as the environmental consequences of the high-energy dissipation life style become well known and accepted by everyone. These benefits will all be part of a greater effort in envirostability in finding sustainable and lower impact living. We must start now.

16

TO GO WHERE NO PERSON HAS GONE BEFORE

As we saw in the last chapter, the future does not look promising. Sometime before the end of this century, we may fry, drown, or get lost in human anthills. An adventurous few will start colonies in the far north.

But there is hope. Optimistic technologists are working on projects to make us hardier and live longer using bioengineering. The movement is called transhumanism. This will give us a great leap forward beyond the glacial pace of evolution. We may even give the coming super robots a run for their money.

Bioengineering

Ray Kurzweil has been focusing much of his future scenarios on bioengineering. He has foreseen all kinds of prosthetic devices for the human body, especially to replace damaged parts including from war wounds. Since his first forecasts, scientists and engineers have recreated human body parts so that now, on paper at least, engineers can assemble a complete "bionic person."

Kurzweil now projects that there will be nanobots embedded in our brains to favorably modify our intelligence and act as immunology agents to destroy pathogens. These nanobots would be real programmed computers about the diameter of a human hair. He commented on the bionic body to the *Wall Street Journal*: "Isn't there a natural limit to how long an automobile will last? However, if you take care of it and if anything goes wrong, you fix it and maybe replace it, it can go on forever."

So what will be the major significance of Kurzweil's bionic people? They might be moved to the hospitable parts of the earth remaining after major global warming and other disasters. Their augmented memories would carry forward the knowledge necessary for future generations to live productively and happily.

An intriguing question is: "Will the Singularity point Kurzweil talks about be moved to a later time as the bionic people may again become smarter than the robots?"

Another approach to life extension is to repair the physical degeneration caused by aging due to the loss of telomeres. These are the DNA segments at the ends of chromosomes. A cell dies when it runs out of telomeres. Researchers at Harvard Medical School have announced that after they administered the associated enzyme called telomerase to mice suffering from aging disorders, the mice effectively became younger.

•••

The next step in DNA engineering could be to use "synthetic biology" to create new or modified organisms. Altering the DNA is the most common approach. A leader in this fledgling science is the entrepreneurial scientist, John Craig Venter. His business, scientific and personal residences are in high tech and wealthy La Jolla, California. He first became well known when his Institute for Genomic Research completed the first genome sequence of a free-living organism, the bacterium *Haemophilus influenzae*. In 1998, he incorporated Celera Genomics to beat the government-funded effort to sequence the human genome, which has three billion chemical units and about 20,500 genes. Both teams jointly announced complete mapping of the genome in 2000 with the final sequence mapped in 2003. In that same year, Venter made the virus phi X 174 synthetically, and in 2010, he made the first synthetic bacterial cell, *Mycoplasma mycoides*. Synthetic Genomics is his latest company.

Venter has concluded that life is a DNA software system. This software creates and directs the construction of proteins and cells. Venter explains we can read the "software of life" by sequencing DNA. He says that if you have rewritten the software of a genome, you have changed life itself. The "DNA software" is analogous to computer software because it includes stored information and instructions to be used in a process. Information can be used, for example, to synthesize proteins, and the DNA software has the mechanisms, including the accompanying messenger RNA, to transport the information where needed. This is very similar to the early digital computers, which used punched paper tape or cards to reference and deliver information according to a program in the computer.

Venter writes in his book, *Life at the Speed of Light: From the Double Helix to the Dawn of Digital Life*, "Now we can go the other direction by starting with the computerized digital code, designing a new life form, chemically synthesizing its DNA, and then booting it up to produce the actual organism. And because the information is now digital, we can send it anywhere at the speed of light and re-create the DNA and life at the other end."

•••

An engaging example of genetic engineering, or synthetic biology, is creating living dinosaurs. Think *Jurassic Park*, the popular 1993 film. Imagine creating a living, breathing, Velociraptor or even a Neanderthal man.

Jurassic Park portrayed extracting dinosaur DNA from mosquitoes embedded for millions of years in amber, the transparent yellow and hardened tree sap. Scientists feel that while this approach might work, the chances of success are very small. One problem is that DNA can only survive for about 6.3 million years or so, and dinosaurs died out 65 million years ago. Another approach, which has more promise, is working backwards from birds. Reversing time, so to speak.

Paleontologists generally agree that birds descended from raptor dinosaurs. McGill University professor Hans Larsson and a former graduate student found that carnivorous dinosaur limb lengths showed a relatively stable scaling relationship with body size. The limb scaling changed when fore- and hind limbs dramatically decoupled from body size, which allowed birds to evolve from the dinosaurs. The hind legs shortened from monster thighs to very short and stick-like. The front legs evolved into wings. The long, heavy tails became residuals and were replaced by fans of feathers. The new bird species, of course, also had to develop hollow bones, small body sizes and high metabolic rates. Some dinosaurs already had feathers.

Their bigger discovery, however, was that the dinosaurs' ancestral DNA is still present in the birds. In 2007, Larsson was examining a chicken embryo and with his microscope could find 16 vertebrae instead of the expected four to eight vertebrae—the bird had a residual reptilian tail. Larsson said, "For about 150 million years, this kind of tail has never existed in birds, but they have always carried it deep in their embryology." Then he decided to see what would happen by manipulating the genetic make-up of the tail. He extended it by another three vertebrae. He had demonstrated a method for turning on dormant dinosaur genes.

A corroborating find was by Matt Harris and John Fallow at the University of Wisconsin in 2005. They found signs of undeveloped teeth in mutant chickens. Harris and Fallow turned-on the "teeth gene" using a triggering virus and their chicken grew the curved teeth like those of a dinosaur. (Can we still say "Scarce as hen's teeth"?) They also programmed the chickens to grow feathers on their legs instead of scales. The dinosaurs' genome, which was mutated to become a bird, could be reversed so a bird could become a dinosaur.

Larsson believes that in a hundred years or sooner geneticists will be able to retro-engineer dinosaurs including the gigantic Tyrannosaurus Rex. All the genetic coding is in the bird.

It is hard to say where this might lead with people. Undoubtedly, the chicken-dinosaur discoveries will stimulate researchers to explore all kinds of genetic programming in humans. The moral issues could delay projects, however, as happened for stem cell research in the United States. Nevertheless, we must recognize that as the living gets ever tougher, with global warming and other problems, the remaining humans will try anything, including all the bioengineering approaches, to improve their lives and the future as best they can.

The Final Frontier

The robots will step out and walk around. They will not care about the local atmospheric composition, if there is water, or the weather. They may even be shot by laser-armed troops, to no avail. They have landed on a promising planet in the Tau Ceti system, 11.9 light years from Earth. In another 11.9 years, the earth will start receiving a stream of reports. Why did this happen? Why robots?

In the first instance, this space project is no different from creating dinosaurs from chickens. We are exploring all spaces inside and outside of our earth cage to discover the unknown, find answers to eternal questions, and to explore lands way out there to see what opportunities of any kind lurk for our exploitation.

Of course, it makes no sense to bring this topic up unless reasonable and informed people think that it is feasible. My opinion is that both projects—putting robots on a planet of Tau Ceti and a human colony on Mars—have little chance of success. Whether either or both should be attempted is another matter. Both will be unimaginably expensive and probably fraught with failed attempts.

I will focus on a few salient aspects of the robotic Tau Ceti mission rather than the often-discussed manned Mars mission. In 1946, Stanislaw Ulam made a proposal to study the concept of propulsion of spacecraft by a series of nuclear explosions ("nuclear pulse propulsion"). Ulam was a distinguished mathematician who was a major contributor to the Manhattan Project at the Los Alamos Laboratory in New Mexico, which developed the atomic bomb. Nuclear reactions provide enormous amounts of energy per mass of fuel used compared to equal masses of chemical propellants. Studies indicated that a thermonuclear (hydrogen bomb technology) spaceship can reach 8% to 10% of the speed of light and a fission (atomic bomb technology) spaceship can reach 3% to 5% of the speed of light (299,000 kilometers or 186,000 miles per second).

The project was named Orion and converted to the feasibility engineering and test stage at the General Atomics facility (later purchased to be a division of General Dynamics) in San Diego, California, in 1958. It was led by physicists Ted Taylor, a specialist in small atomic bombs, from the Los Alamos Laboratory, and Freeman Dyson from the Institute for Advanced Study in Princeton, New Jersey.

Dyson calculated a thermonuclear spaceship would need 44 years to reach Alpha Centauri, a three-star system about 4.3 light years away. Therefore, reaching Tau Ceti where life is more likely to be found, would take about 122 years with the same spaceship design—longer the any person's lifetime.

The Orion project continued with optimism, and some components were tested using conventional explosives at Point Loma, San Diego, in 1959. The project was terminated in 1964 in conformance with the Partial Test Ban Treaty of 1963. Much of the concern was about atmospheric radiation hazards associated with ground-launched schemes.

•••

The science and engineering that supported Project Orion could be used to develop design for better living on an increasing less bountiful and less comfortable earth. One can imagine, for example, living modules patterned roughly after today's mobile homes but which could be stacked to make high-density housing. These modules would include integrated video and computer equipment, cooking and washing systems predesigned to work well with household robots, food modules such as aquaponic systems for growing vegetables and fish in one enclosed aquatic system, water and waste-recycling systems, and snap-on solar energy arrays. Everything would be as beautifully designed and seamlessly integrated as the consoles of today's cars and the features of smart phones. Inventing and engineering the smartphone over its many generations and including components probably took as many person-hours.

Commenting on the need to solve really big problems, Buzz Aldrin, one of the two astronauts on the first team to walk on the moon, said: "You promised me Mars colonies. Instead, I got Facebook." As I write, Facebook has a market value of about $173 billion.

The challenges that face us and solving them brings to mind President Kennedy's words at Rice University in 1962:

> But why, some say, the moon? Why choose this as our goal?...Why climb the highest mountain? Why, 35 years ago, fly the Atlantic?...We choose to go to the moon in this decade and do the other things, not because they are easy, but because they are hard; because that goal will serve to organize and measure the best of our energies and skills...

So we can work on prolonging life, making hardier people, developing robots that are commercial and life partners, and traveling to possibly better places, far and near. But we will not be content and optimistic again until we find a stable equilibrium with all our environmental elements. We must consider all elements from the smallest of creatures to the greenhouse gasses above. Everything must work together as a stable system, including us. We will have reached envirostability.

17

A NEW BEGINNING

Bright New Era or Societal Collapse?

We are living in an era of profound transformations. This is the time when there are unprecedented environmental changes. Meanwhile we are trying to reconcile human intelligence with machine intelligence. The old economic models like free enterprise capitalism are increasingly being questioned in terms of eliminating massive poverty or sustainability in view of exporting jobs, automation, and disappearing resources.

The human species, with its capabilities as programmed in its genes, may be achieving well below its possibilities. Our demise will be because the enemy we cannot control is us, not robots or terrorists in distant lands. We may be heading towards the winter of the genomes. Many of the animal and plant species will be threatened or newly extinct, so it also could be their winter also.

After researching why some societies make disastrous decisions, Jared Diamond, summarized his findings as: "Failure to anticipate a problem, failure to perceive it once it has arisen, failure to attempt to solve it after it has been perceived, and failure to succeed in attempts to solve it." Right now, in the western world, we are at stage three where we flailing about in attempts to deal with the problems discussed in this book.

Diamond goes on, "Today, just as in the past, countries that are environmentally stressed, overpopulated, or both, become at risk of getting politically stressed, and of their governments collapsing...(People) try to emigrate at any cost. They fight each other over land. They kill each other. They start civil wars. They figure that they have nothing to lose, so they become terrorists, or they support terrorism....The results of these transparent connections are genocides..." Does this seem eerily similar to various countries in the Mideast today? Since we do not want problems to be solved by war, genocide, epidemics or societal collapse, we must be thinking now about how to move ahead constructively.

The world faces a "bottleneck of overpopulation and wasteful consumption" that could drive many of Earth's species to extinction in this century, according to E.O. Wilson. He adds, "We're in the end game all around the world," and "The greatest challenge, I believe, is to raise the quality of life of people everywhere while also pulling through the rest of life with us before we come out the other end."

After we go through the Big Squeeze, several general scenarios about the human condition can be envisioned:

1 - Society goes on more or less like now except that there will be far fewer people. Population decline will happen one way or another. Consumption and standards of living probably will decline led by standards of sustainability and envirostability.

2 - The human population survives but higher culture, fine arts, technologies and detailed process know-how are lost probably forever. People have become self-absorbed and at the same time, the lights go out in the electronic world. Another Dark Age settles in.

3 - A "post-human" culture takes hold. Bionic people have a symbiotic intellectual alliance with their computers and the data clouds. Brain conditioning and stimulation becomes the highest priority. The bionic people may become bored, however, and conclude that Earth has run out of possibilities. On the other hand, they may find new energy and develop new ways to restart man's quest for the sustainable good life.

So what do we do? Let us assume that Earth can save itself through evolution, but there will be a new environment with a different climate and a different composition of species. Man will have to get creative to live in that environment. We will have to start over, using our intellectual resources.

A starting point is to reset our minds to Albert Einstein's famous observation:

The most beautiful experience we can have is the mysterious. It is the fundamental emotion which stands at the cradle of true art and true science. Whoever does not know it and can no longer wonder, no longer marvel, is as good as dead, and his eyes are dimmed.

•••

Daring to explore the mysterious requires new ideas and knowledge. This begins the creative process leading to new art, science, innovation and economic development. This is what AI and robots cannot do.

Education is foremost here. Four things need to be done:

1 – Get children interested in creative accomplishment at an early age and keep them focused on this throughout their lifetimes. This requires teachers who love what they are doing. Teachers who are on fire. Teachers who love math, science, art, history and literature. Teachers who really want their students to absorb what they are taught.

2 – Make sure that the fundamental knowledge needed has been presented and learned. Prospective creativity and invention will not flourish or be carried to fruition if students do not learn reading, writing, history, math and the sciences.

3 – See that the students who are interested in innovation, invention and entrepreneurship do not drop out of school prematurely, foregoing the additional technical education and communications and social skills that they will need.

4 – Open the students' eyes to the necessity of harmony with the environment. They must adapt to the environment, to the balance of nature, and through this reduce many of their tensions and anxieties and expand their understanding of how everything fits together.

We will need many graduates who are hooked by the challenge of the unknown. They will be captivated by the wonder of unknown and the goal of making a unique contribution to its understanding. They should think of our world as people, insects, animals, plants and resources living in dynamic relationships.

All organisms change by evolution forced upon them by a changing biosphere. Now we have introduced the new species, which is a huge variety of computers. They will fit in with every-thing else, hopefully in a symbiotic relationship with humans that will be good for everybody. This should be taught at the earliest possible time in schools.

Continuing education for adults is more important than ever because technology and its applications are changing so rapidly. An adult can change job specialties or careers three or more times in a lifetime. Fortunately, career-based education is easily accessible with community colleges, online courses and other easy-to-use offerings.

The motivational process starts at the top—with the President of the United States—and carries through political and business leaders, parents, clergy, educators and many oth-ers. When Russia launched the first orbiting satellite, there was frenzy in the United States not to fall behind in the techno-logical race. We put our man on the moon first, and this goal has faded out. Now the world is facing larger and sometimes irreversible problems of environment, climate, food, water and energy. We must develop a new sense of mission.

Computer, AI and Robots

I have talked a lot in this book about almost all aspects of artificial intelligence technology. It makes much of our current economy, culture and lifestyle possible. It may even help in minimizing global warming. But I detect a great fear of the coming wave of super-smart computers and robots. People often tell me that they think computers will never be as smart as we are, but they are also afraid that computers will take over some day. This is a contradiction, but maybe it is also a sign of the classical human reaction to think of man as the center of all things.

The essence of the matter is that humans do some things much better than computers, and these are things that require curiosity, imagination, sensitivity, and emotion. We can think of art and deep sciences calling for these attributes.

Computers, on the other hand, can flawlessly process volumes of data beyond any amount that we can imagine. The real threat to freedom and its attendant happiness happens when a power-obsessed human is combined with a gigantic super intelligent computer. Big Brother has arrived.

This alliance overwhelms us so we do not know where the truth ends and fiction begins. Information is both sucked from the population and is rained down upon it. Answers that are apparently right because "everyone knows" substitute for science. In non-reversible, catastrophic phenomena like climate change, truth must trump belief.

As we get older, almost all of us yearn for the carefree times of childhood. The child has the almost naïve capability of unfettered imagination. Some people, very few, keep this imaginative ability through adulthood. Their imaginings lead to inventions, art, designs and explorations of frontiers never seen before. Emotion is part of this creativity, and perhaps the emotional element is what is hardest to reconcile in equating the human mind to an advanced computer.

Machines will continue to develop as evolutionary beings. They may become self-aware and self-improving. In time, they could develop emotion and conscience. They will coexist with humans along with all the other creatures and resources of the ecosphere.

I believe it is safe to say that the greatest threat to humankind is not computers gone mad, but humans who aspire to be like God and to reach Godly heights by their acquisitive powers and inventions, including using ever smarter and dominant computers.

Towards the New Frontier

Times of insight and creativity come and go with the ebb and flow of unexploited knowledge and with society's sense of urgency for new solutions. The industrial revolution and World War II were eras that saw surges of insights, creativity and invention. Now the world is benefitting from a combination of bright new minds coming up through the educational systems, well-equipped laboratories and shops, and the new information sources of the computer clouds; but there is an apocalyptic sense of the world running out of time. Many people feel a sense of "Why bother?" because it appears that the world has run out of possibilities.

People must see that virtually all knowledge and data is available to them and that creativity has never been more important than now. Children should be encouraged to expect that there is an infinite future for them. Society's failure is failure to give them hope and encouragement. Children are the future.

Now is the time for the men and women who dream of things that never were. Their dreams and visions are the starting points in great creations and in solving apparently unsolvable problems. The positive emotions will energize everyone. Winter of the genomes? I say "no!" Not if mankind shakes off apathy, avoids political barriers, and fearlessly explores the frontier ahead. The challenge will be both intellectual and physical. Not even the sky is the limit.

GLOSSARY

Albedo. The amount of sunlight reflected by a planetary surface.

AI. (see artificial intelligence)

Algorithm. A set of instructions to carry out carry out a procedure or process. It is usually in the form of a computer program derived from a set of equations or a flow diagram.

Android. A robot in the form of a human being.

Artificial Intelligence (AI). The ability of a computer or other machine to perform those activities that are normally thought to require intelligence. Artificial intelligence devices range from bug-like robots that can find their way around a terrain to mega-computers that someday may be more intelligent than humans. The term artificial intelligence is used in a variety of ways ranging from an engineering and scientific discipline to a specific computer, program or device.

Associative Inference. Calculating or inferring the strength of the connection between two words or data points in a knowledge network such as a computer data base or a network of neurons. While all points are usually connected to each other, the strength of any given relationship is determined by the sum of the strengths of the direct and indirect connections between the two data points. Example: "dog" and "ice" would not be likely to have a strong connection, but "dog" and "fur" would have a very strong connection based on direct and indirect (multi-linkage) connections.

Avatar. An image or model that represents a person. Sometimes a genetically matched human being controls it.

Bioengineering. The application of engineering to medicine, biology and physiology including the production of artificial limbs and organs.

Bionic. Augmenting the strength or intelligence of a human by the inclusion of electronic or mechanical devices. Often means creating superhuman strength, intelligence or longevity.

Biosphere. The ecosystem of the earth and the living organisms together with their environment.

Chromosome. Rod or threadlike DNA-containing structures that carry the genes in a linear order. The human genome has 23 pairs of chromosomes, one from each parent, including the X and Y for the female and male chromosomes. Females are X-X; males are X-Y.

Clouds, computer clouds. An evolving term referring to computer services accessed in the Internet, especially where there are extremely large capacities of programs and data storage. The user generally does not need to know about the technology of the computers, software or data handling.

Cognitive Information processing. Computer theory and devices designed to replicate cognitive thinking such as done by humans. A device has sensory inputs and short- and long-term memories. Much of the development in this area is done with associative inference and neuronal chips that are similar to arrays of synapses.

Cyborg. A person whose body contains mechanical or electrical devices to enhance capabilities and powers.

DNA. A nucleic acid that is the basic building block of chromosomes. The DNA molecule consists of two polynucleotide chains in the form of a double helix. Sequences of DNA called genes provide the coding leading to protein synthesis and the transmission of hereditary characteristics.

Envirostability. The stability of the relationship of nature, Earth, the environment, man, and machines.

GAIA Theory. "A view of the earth introduced in the 1980s that sees it as a self-regulating system made up of the totality of organisms, the surface rocks, the ocean and the atmosphere tightly coupled as an evolving system." (James Lovelock, *The Vanishing face of GAIA,* Basic Books, New York, 209).

Gene. The basic unit of heredity. A specific sequence of nucleotides in DNA, usually located on a chromosome, which provide the instructions for the synthesis of RNA. It, in turn, when translated to a protein, results in the expression of a hereditary characteristic. The human genome contains approximately 20,000 genes.

Genome. The genome is the complete set of genetic information for an organism. The human genome has 23 chromosomes. The human genome contains approximately 20,000 protein-coding genes.

Greenhouse Effect. An atmospheric heating phenomenon whereby the sun's energy reflected from the earth as infrared radiation energy is trapped by a layer of gases above the Earth's surface. These gases include carbon dioxide, methane and water vapor.

IPCC. The Intergovernmental Panel on Climate Change (IPCC) is a scientific body operating under the auspices of the United Nations. The IPCC does not carry out its own research, nor does it monitor climate change itself. Its work is done by scientist volunteers, analyzing published literature, and whose reports are reviewed by the governments of more than 120 countries. Its work and that of NASA are generally considered the acknowledged authorities for policy makers.

Knowosphere. All of the available electronically stored information in the world that is accessible by search engines or may be found through social media.

Moore's Law. A statement that technology tends to improve exponentially. Gordon Moore observed that improvements in miniaturization led to a doubling of the number of transistors on an integrated circuit chip every 18 months (variations of the statement range from 12 to 24 months).

Robot. A machine that is controlled by a computer and sometimes by a person or other computer. It is often made to look like a human or animal. Robots generally fall within the category of artificially intelligent devices.

Transcendent. Going beyond ordinary limits or experience. To head for or reach a superior or supreme state.

Transhuman. An intermediary form between human and post human or cyborg. A transhuman resembles a human but has additional powers and abilities.

Turing Test. A proposed test by the mathematician Alan Turing to demonstrate that a machine is intelligent. If a human cannot tell which responses from a human and from a machine to common inquiries and conversation are from the human or the machine, then the machine has passed the test and can be described as intelligent. This controversial test is widely encountered in artificial intelligence discussions.

Sentience. Feeling, sensation, absorbing external stimulation.

Sentient machine. Not precisely defined yet, but used in the media to mean a computer that has self-awareness and artificial general intelligence.

Singularity. A term made popular by Ray Kurzweil who has defined his use of it as: "The Singularity will represent the culmination of the merger of our biological thinking and existence with our technology, resulting in a world that is human but transcends our biological roots." (Ray Kurzweil, *The Singularity is Near*, Penguin, New York, 2005). In an interview about that book, Kurzweil said: "We'll get to a point where technical progress will be so fast that unenhanced human intelligence will be unable to follow it. That will mark the Singularity." Singularity is often described as the point in time when computer intelligence exceeds human intelligence. Kurzweil forecasted this point to be 2045.

Synaptic Processor. Uses associative information processing with electronic synapses and massively parallel processing. Energy consumption is minimal. Used experimentally to do human-like computing. This is the alternate architecture to the conventional Von Neumann architecture.

Synthetic Biology. The science of altering genetics including by using gene manipulation and computer science techniques to create organism variations or artificial biological systems.

Von Neumann architecture. The original and predominant digital computer architecture in which computers are constructed by separating memory and processing and operate by executing a series of equations or algorithms. Alternate computer architectures are sought where there is massively parallel real-time data inputs (such as from the eyes, ears, nose, and touch), where the algorithms are not fully known nor need to be fully understood, and the energy consumed by the computer must be kept to a minimum (see Synaptic Processor above).

REFERENCES

Introduction

Gillis, Justin, "Climate Efforts Falling Short, U.N. Panel Says," *New York Times*, April 13, 2014, http://www.nytimes.com/2014/04/14/science/earth/un-climate-panel-warns-speedier-action-is-needed-to-avert-disaster.html?_r=0.

Jordans, Frank, "UN Climate Change Panel to Discuss Global Transition to Renewable Energy," *Renewable EnergyWorld.com*, April 9, 2014, http://www.renewableenergyworld.com/rea/news/article/2014/04/un-climate-change-panel-to-discuss-global-transition-from-fossil-to-renewable-energy.

World fertility rates and population statistics:
United Nations, http://www.un.org/en/development/desa/population/.
World Bank, http://data.worldbank.org/indicator/SP.DYN.TFRT.IN.
Total Fertility Rate, Wikipedia, http://en.wikipedia.org/wiki/Total_fertility_rate.

Chapter 1 Man and Machines

Arthur, Brian, "The Second Economy," http://www.mckinsey-quarterly.com/The_second_economy_2853.

Asimov, Issac, *I, Robot,* Spectra, New York, 2004.

Darwin, Charles, *The Origin of Species,* Signet Classics, New York, 2003.

Frey, Carl Benedikt and Osborn, Michael A., "The Future of Employment: How Susceptible are Jobs to Computerisation?" Oxford University Working Paper, http://www.futuretech.ox.ac.uk/sites/futuretech.ox.ac.uk/files/The_Future_of_Employment_OMS_Working_Paper_1.pdf.

Greenfield, Susan, from "We are the Final Frontier," by Ian Sample, *The Guardian,* February 10, 2005, guardian.co.uk. http://www.theguardian.com/education/2005/feb/10/science.highereducation.

Guizzo, Erico, "World's Robot Population and More Stats," *IEEE Spectrum,* March 21, 2008, http://spectrum.ieee.org/automaton/robotics/robotics-software/world_robot_population_and_more_stats.

Her, a commercial movie exploring a man's relationship with a female software program (2014).

IFR International federation of Robotics, Statistical Department, *World Robotics,* http://www.worldrobotics.org/index.php?id=100.

Kilham, Larry, *MegaMinds: How to Create and Invent in the Age of Google*, Amazon Kindle, 2010.

Kurzweil, Ray, "The Life Robotic," Interview with Andrew Goldman, *New York Times Magazine*, January 27, 2013, p. 12.

Kurzweil, Ray, *The Singularity is Near: When Humans Transcend*, Penguin Books, New York, 2005.

Turkle, Sherry, *Alone Together: Why We Expect More from Technology and Less from Each Other*, Basic Books, New York, 2011.

Robot & Frank, Commercial movie about a retired man and his helper robot (2012). Light hearted but insightful.

Watson, J.D. and Crick, F.H.C., "A Structure for Deoxyribose Nucleic Acid," *Nature* 171, 1953, pp. 737-38. http://www.nature.com/nature/dna50/watsoncrick.pdf.

Chapter 2 Crisis of the Bees

Bekoff, Marc, "The Birds and the Bees and Their Brains: Size Doesn't Matter," *Psychology Today*, April 5, 2013, http://www.psychologytoday.com/blog/animal-emotions/201304/the-birds-and-the-bees-and-their-brains-size-doesnt-matter.

Cohen, Joel E., *How Many People Can the Earth Support?* W.W. Norton & Company, New York, 1995.

Falconer, Jason, "Harvard's flying robot insect can now hover and steer," *Gizmag.com*, May 8, 2013, http://www.gizmag.com/harvard-robobee-flying-robot-insect/27432/.

The Green Brain Project, The University of Sheffield, UK. http://greenbrain.group.shef.ac.uk/.

Lovejoy, Thomas, "A Tsunami of Extinction," *Scientific American*, January, 2013, pp. 33-34, http://www.scientificamerican.com/article.cfm?id=extinction-countdown-end-for-many-species.

Pettis, Jeffery S., et al, "Crop Pollination Exposes Honey Bees to Pesticides Which Alters Their Susceptibility to the Gut Pathogen *Nosema Ceranae*," *PLOS ONE*, July 24, 2013, http://www.plosone.org/article/info:doi/10.1371/journal.pone.0070182.

Red List of Threatened Species, The International Union for Conservation of Nature (IUCN), http://www.iucnredlist.org/about/summary-statistics.

Robobee, Wikipedia, http://en.wikipedia.org/wiki/RoboBee.

"RoboBees to the Rescue," PBS *Nova*, October 3, 201, http://www.pbs.org/wgbh/nova/tech/robobees-rescue.html.

"Robotic insects make first controlled flight," *Harvard School of Engineering and Applied Sciences*, May 2, 2013, http://www.seas.harvard.edu/news/2013/05/robotic-insects-make-first-controlled-flight.

Walsh, Bryan, "A World Without Bees," *Time,* August 19, 2013, pp. 25-31, http://science.time.com/2013/08/09/the-trouble-with-beekeeping-in-the-anthropocene/.

Wilson, E.O., *The Diversity of Species,* W.W. Norton & Company, New York, 1992.

Wilson, E.O., "Is Humanity Suicidal?" *New York Times Magazine,* May 30, 1993, pp. 23-29. http://www.mysterium.com/suicidal.html.

Wood, Robert; Nagpal, Radhika; and Wei, Gu-Yeon, "The Robobee Project is Building Flying Robots the Size of Insects," *Scientific American,* May 11, 2013, http://www.scientificamerican.com/article.cfm?id=robobee-project-building-flying-robots-insect-size.

Chapter 3 What is Artificial Intelligence?

Gelernter, David, "Artificial Intelligence Is Lost in the Woods," *Technology Review,* July/August 2007, http://www.technologyreview.com/article/408171/artificial-intelligence-is-lost-in-the-woods/.

IBM Corporation. "IBM Unveils Cognitive Computer Chips," August 18, 2011, http://www-03.ibm.com/press/us/en/pressrelease/35251.wss.
See also, Simonite, Tom, "Thinking in Silicon," *MIT Technology Review,* January, 2014, http://m.technologyreview.com/featuredstory/522476/thinking-in-silicon/#.UtLxFQENdbw.gmail.

Koza, John R., Keane, Martin A., and Streeter, Matthew J., "Evolving Inventions," *Scientific American,* February 2003, pp. 52-59, http://www.scientificamerican.com/article/evolving-inventions/.
For more on John Koza's projects, see http://www.genetic-programming.com/.

Kurzweil, Ray. *The Singularity is Near: When Humans Transcend Biology,* Penguin Books, New York, 2005.

Lehrer, Jonah, "Out of the Blue," *Seed Magazine,* March 3, 2008. http://seedmagazine.com/content/article/out_of_the_blue/.

Markoff, John, "Brainlike Computers, Learning From Experience," *The New York Times,* December 28, 2013, http://www.nytimes.com/2013/12/29/science/brainlike-computers-learning-from-experience.html?pagewanted=all&_r=0.

Markoff, John, "IBM Develops a New Chip That Functions Like a Brain," *The New York Times,* August 7, 2014, http://www.nytimes.com/2014/08/08/science/new-computer-chip-is-designed-to-work-like-the-brain.html?emc=edit_th_20140808&nl=todaysheadlines&nlid=58190540&_r=0.

Markram, Henry, "The Blue Brain Project," *Nature Reviews, Neuroscience,* 7, February 2006, pp 153-160, http://en.wikipedia.org/wiki/Blue_Brain_Project.

McCorduck, Pamela, *Machines Who Think,* A K Peters, Natick, Mass., Revised edition, 2004. (Comprehensive overall review of artificial intelligence.)

Merolla, P.A. et al. "A million spiking-neuron integrated circuit with a scalable communication network and interface," Science, Vol. 345 no. 6197 DOI: 10.1126/science.1254642, http://www.sciencemag.org/content/345/6197/668.full.

Minsky, Marvin, *The Emotion Machine,* Simon & Schuster Paperbacks, New York, 2007 (New perspectives on artificial intelligence).

"The Rise of Artificial Intelligence and Its Potiential Effects on Business," (very good overview 8 minute video), http://www.technology-in-business.net/the-rise-of-artificial-intelligence-and-its-effects-on-business/.

"Watson (computer)," http://en.wikipedia.org/wiki/Watson_ (computer).

Chapter 4 AI and Living Beings

Hauser, Marc, *Wild Minds: What Animals really Think,* Henry Holt, New York, 2000.

The Human Brain Project, https://www.humanbrainproject.eu.

Kilham, Larry, *MegaMinds: How to Create and Invent in the Age of Google,* Amazon Kindle, 2010.

Koch, Christof, "Ubiquitous Minds," *Scientific American Mind,* January/February, 2014, http://www.nature.com/

scientificamericanmind/journal/v25/n1/full/scientificameri-canmind0114-26.html.

Kurzweil, Ray, *How to Create a Mind*, Viking, New York, 2012. For this chapter, see chapter 8, "The Mind as Computer."

Legged Squad Support System (LS3) combat support robots, Boston Dynamics, http://bostondynamics.com.

National Institute of Informatics (Japan), *Informatics Studies and Projects*, http://www.nii.ac.jp/en/research/informatics/.

Worm brain simulation, http://www.openworm.org/.

Russell, Peter, "The evolution of Consciousness," http://www.peterrussell.com/SCG/EoC.php.

Zimmer, Carl, "In the Human Brain, Size Really Isn't Everything," *The New York Times*, December 26, 2013, http://www.nytimes.com/2013/12/26/science/in-the-human-brain-size-really-isnt-everything.html?_r=0&pagewanted=print.

Chapter 5 The Quiet Invasion of AI and Robots

Automated product and service communication packages, London Brand Management, London, U.K. http://www.londonbrandmanagement.com.

Davidson, Adam, "Skills Don't Pay the Bills," *New York Times Magazine*, Nov. 20, 2012, http://www.nytimes.com/2012/11/25/magazine/skills-dont-pay-the-bills.html?pagewanted=all&_r=0.

"Domestic Robot Design for Older Adults Enables 'Aging in Place,'" Georgia Tech GVU Center, https://gvu.gatech.edu/news/2012-04-02/domestic-robot-design-older-adults-enables-aging-place?destination=node/1686.

IFR International federation of Robotics, Statistical Department, *World Robotics*, http://www.worldrobotics.org/index.php?id=100.

"A Robot for the Rest of Us," *Machine Design*, October 18, 2012, http://machinedesign.com/robotics/baxter-robot-rest-us.

Eitel, Elizabeth, "Robots Priced for the Masses," *Machine Design*, January 16, 2014, http://machinedesign.com/robotics/technology-forecast-2014-robots-priced-masses.

Markoff, John, "Skilled Work Without the Worker," *New York Times*, August 18, 2012,
http://www.nytimes.com/2012/08/19/business/new-wave-of-adept-robots-is-changing-global-industry.html?pagewanted=all.

Narrative Science company, Quill software, http://narrativescience.com.

Turkle, Sherry, *Alone Together: Why We Expect More from Technology and Less from Each Other*, Basic Books, New York, 2011.

Wakefield, Jane, " Singularity: The robots are coming to steal our jobs," *BBC Online*, January 12, 2014,
http://www.bbc.co.uk/news/technology-25000756.

Chapter 6 Employment Consequences
of the AI and Robot Invasion

Brynjolfsson, Erik and McAfee, Andrew, *Race Against the Machine*, Digital Frontier Press, 2011.

Frey, Carl Benedikt and Osborne, Michael, A., "The Future of Employment: How Susceptible are Jobs to Computerisation?" Oxford University, UK, September 17, 2013, http://www.futuretech.ox.ac.uk/sites/futuretech.ox.ac.uk/files/The_Future_of_Employment_OMS_Working_Paper_0.pdf.

Gordon, Robert J., "Is U.S. Economic Growth Over? Faltering Innovation Confronts the Six Headwinds," Working Paper 18315, http://faculty-web.at.northwestern.edu/economics/gordon../Is US Economic Growth Over.pdf.

Krugman, Paul, "Is Growth Over?" Blog in *New York Times*, December 26, 2012, http://krugman.blogs.nytimes.com/2012/12/26/is-growth-over/.

Kuo, Lily, "Japan Is Counting on Friendly Robots to Save Its Economy," *The Atlantic*, June 27, 2013, http://www.theatlantic.com/business/archive/2013/06/japan-is-counting-on-friendly-robots-to-save-its-economy/277290/.

Turkle, Sherry, *Alone Together: Why We Expect More from Technology and Less from Each Other*, Basic Books, New York, 2011.

Von Drehle, David, "The Robot Economy," *Time*, September 9, 2013, http://content.time.com/time/magazine/article/0,9171,2150607,00.html.

Chapter 7 The Challenge for Education

Gorniak-Kocikowska, Krystyna, interview with Jim Shelton, *New Haven Register*, "SCSU professor has her eye on the robot revolution," February 15, 2014. http://www.nhregister.com/general-news/20140215/scsu-professor-has-her-eye-on-the-robot-revolution.

Koller, Frank, Interview with Paul Solman, "Man vs. Machine," Making Sen$e report, 2012, PBS Newshour, http://www.pbs.org/newshour/making-sense/should-we-fear-the-end-of-work/.
Momentum Machines, producers of burger-bots, http://momentummachines.com/.
See also:
Roush, Wade, "Hamburger, Coffee, Guitars, and Cars: A Report from Lemnos Labs," *Xconomy.com (enewsletter)*, June 12, 2012, http://www.xconomy.com/san-francisco/2012/06/12/hamburgers-coffee-guitars-and-cars-a-report-from-lemnos-labs/.
And:
Dorier, Jason, "Burger Robot Poised to Disrupt Fast Food Industry," *SingularityHub.com* (enews letter), August 10, 2014. http://singularityhub.com/2014/08/10/burger-robot-poised-to-disrupt-fast-food-industry/.

Reif, Rafael L., "Online learning will make college cheaper. It will also make it better," *Time*, September 26, 2013, http://nation.time.com/2013/09/26/online-learning-will-make-college-cheaper-it-will-also-make-it-better/.

Smith, Nancy Duvergne, "MIT Living Wage Calculator: Why Higher Wages Help Everybody," https://alum.mit.edu/pages/sliceofmit/2014/02/06/mit-living-wage-calculator-why-higher-wages-help-everybody/?test=1966477630.

Chapter 8 Population and Fertility Issues

Adsera, Alicia, *Vanishing Children: From High Unemployment to Low Fertility in Developed Countries*, Princeton, May, 2005. *https:// www.princeton.edu/~adsera/AER05_Final.pdf.*

Becker, Gary S., "An Economic Analysis of Fertility," *Demographic and Economic Change in Developed Countries*, pp. 209-240, Columbia University Press, New York. Chapter URL, http:// www.nber.org/chapters/c2387.pdf.

Cohen, Joel E., *How Many People Can the Earth Suport?*, W.W. Norton & Co., New York, 1995.

"Fertility rates affected by global economic crisis," International Institute for Applied Systems Analysis (IIASA), Laxenburg, Austria, June, 2011. http://www.iiasa.ac.at/web/home/about/ news/current/Fertility-rates-affected-by-global-economic- crisis.html.

Frey, Carl Benedikt and Osborn, Michael A., "The Future of Employment: How Susceptible are Jobs to Computerisation?" Oxford University Working Paper, http://www.futuretech. ox.ac.uk/sites/futuretech.ox.ac.uk/files/The_Future_of_ Employment_OMS_Working_Paper_1.pdf.

Kim, Doo-Sub, "Theoretical Explanations of Rapid Fertility Decline in Korea," *Japanese Journal of Population*, Vol. 3, No 1, June 2005. http://www.ipss.go.jp/webj-ad/webjournal.files/popula- tion/2005_6/kim.pdf.

Lovelock, James, *The Vanishing Face of Gaia*, Basic Books, New York, 2009.

Malthusian Trap, *Wikipedia*, http://en.wikipedia.org/wiki/Malthusian_trap.

Mayhew, Robert J., *Malthus*, The Belknap Press of the Harvard University Press, Cambridge, Mass. and London, 2014.

Porter, Eduardo, "Reducing Carbon by Curbing Population," *New York Times*, August 5, 2014, http://www.nytimes.com/2014/08/06/business/economy/population-curbs-as-a-means-to-cut-carbon-emissions.html?_r=0.

Schaller, Jessamyn, "Booms, Busts, and Fertility: Testing the Becker Model Using Gender-Specific Labor Demand," University of California in Davis, 2012.

Teitelbaum, Michael S. and Winter, Jay M., "Bye-Bye, Baby," *New York Times*, March 6, 2014. http://www.nytimes.com/2014/04/05/opinion/sunday/bye-bye-baby.html?_r=0.

Teitelbaum, Michael S. and Winter, Jay. M. *The Global Spread of Fertility Decline: Population, Fear, and Uncertainty*, Yale University Press, New Haven, 2013.

Thomas Robert Malthus, *Wikipedia*, http://en.wikipedia.org/wiki/Thomas_Robert_Malthus.

Wikipedia, "Total Fertility Rate," http://en.wikipedia.org/wiki/Total_fertility_rate.

Wikipedia, "World Population," http://en.wikipedia.org/wiki/World_population.

Wikipedia, "List of Sovereign States and Dependent Territories by Fertility Rate," http://en.wikipedia.org/wiki/List_of_sovereign_states_and_dependent_territories_by_fertility_rate.

World Bank, "Fertility rates, total," http://data.worldbank.org/indicator/sp.dyn.tfrt.in.

Chapter 9 The Age of Robots

Morris, Eric, "From Horse Power to Horse Power," *Access*, Number 30, Spring 2007, http://www.uctc.net/access/30/Access 30 - 02 - Horse Power.pdf.

Brynjolfsson, Erik and McAfee, Andrew, *The Second Machine Age*, W.W. Norton & Co., New York, 2014.

Chapter 10 Robots and Energy

Energy Consumption by Country. http://www.nationmaster.com/country-info/stats/Energy/Energy-use/Kt-of-oil-equivalent.
Also, http://www.nationmaster.com/country-info/stats/Energy/Usage-per-person.

Jordans, Frank, "UN Climate Change Panel to Discuss Global Transition to Renewable Energy," *Renewable EnergyWorld.com*, April 9, 2014, http://www.renewableenergyworld.com/rea/

news/article/2014/04/un-climate-change-panel-to-discuss-global-transition-from-fossil-to-renewable-energy.

Noif, Shimon Y., Editor, *Handbook of Industrial Robotics*, Wiley, New York, 1999.

O'Neill, Brian C., et. al., "Global Demographic Trends and Future Carbon Emissions," *Proceedings of the National Academy of Sciences of the United States of America*, August 27, 2010, http://www.pnas.org/content/early/2010/09/30/1004581107.full.pdf+html.

"Service Robotics Statistics," *International Federation of Robotics (IFR)*, http://www.ifr.org/service-robots/statistics/.

Chapter 11 How Smart Do Robots Need to Be?

"Robots with Feelings." Alice, a robot, recognizes human emotions, University of Augsburg, Germany. An interesting video showing Alice in conversation perceiving and showing basic emotions: http://www.dw.de/robots-with-feelings/av-17547632.

Harris, Tom, "How Robots Work," *HowStuffWorks.com*, April 16, 2002, http://science.howstuffworks.com/robot.htm.

Kilham, Larry, *Love Byte*, Amazon Kindle, 2012.

Kizmet the robot, http://en.wikipedia.org/wiki/Kismet_(robot).

Lamb, Robert, "How have robots changed manufacturing?" *HowStuffWorks.com*, November 10, 2010, http://science.howstuffworks.com/robots-changed-manufacturing.htm.

Layton, Julia, "How Robotic Vacuums Work," *HowStuffWorks.com*, November 3, 2005, http://electronics.howstuffworks.com/gadgets/home/robotic-vacuum.htm.

Morell, Virginia, *Animal Wise: The Thoughts and Emotions of Our Fellow Creatures*, Crown Publishers, New York, 2013.

Chapter 12 Climate Change

Biello, David, "The Little Volcanoes That Could," *Scientific American*, May 1, 2014, http://www.scientificamerican.com/article/volcanoes-that-act-as-air-conditioning-for-a-warming-world/.

Cherry, Steven, "With better software, office buildings can cut energy use by 30 percent," *IEEE Spectrum*, March 12, 2013, http://spectrum.ieee.org/podcast/at-work/test-and-measurement/with-better-software-office-buildings-can-cut-energy-use-by-30-percent.

Erdman, John, "What's a Polar Vortex? The Science Behind Arctic Outbreaks," *The Weather Underground*, http://www.wunderground.com/news/polar-vortex-plunge-science-behind-arctic-cold-outbreaks-20140106.

Fischetti, Mark, "What is This 'Polar Vortex' That is Freezing the U.S.?" *Scientific American* Blog, http://blogs.

scientificamerican.com/observations/2014/01/06/what-is-this-polar-vortex-that-is-freezing-the-u-s/.

"Growth powers clean and green machine," *China Daily,* April 21, 2014, http://www.ecns.cn/business/2014/04-21/110373. shtml.

"Roadmap for moving to a low-carbon economy in 2050," *European Commission, Climate Action.* http://ec.europa.eu/ clima/policies/roadmap/studies_en.htm.

Santer, Benjamin D., et al, "Volcanic contribution to decadal changes in tropospheric temperature," *Nature Geoscience,* February 23, 2014, http://www.nature.com/ngeo/journal/ v7/n3/full/ngeo2098.html.

"Stratospheric Sulfate Aerosols," Wikipedia, http:// en.wikipedia.org/wiki/Stratospheric_sulfate_aerosols_ (geoengineering).

Union of Concerned Scientists, "Global Climate Hot Map," http://www.climatehotmap.org/.

Chapter 13 Robots and Food

"Agricultural Robots – Market Shares, Strategies, and Forecasts, Worldwide, 2014 to 2020," WinterGreen Research, Rockville, Maryland, January 28, 20154, http://www.marketresearch. com/Wintergreen-Research-v739/Agricultural-Robots-Shares-Strategies-Forecasts-8005904/.

Cassidy, Emily S. et al, "Redefining agricultural yields: from tones to people nourished per hectare," *Environmental Research Letters*, August 1, 2013, http://iopscience.iop.org/1748-9326/8/3/034015.

Concepts of Robotic Milking, see http://www.lely.com/en/farming-tips/farming-support/concept-of-robotic-milking.

Webber, Michael E., "How to Make the Food System More Energy Efficient," *Scientific American*, January, 2012, http://www.scientificamerican.com/article/more-food-less-energy/.

Wozniacka, Gosia and Chea, Terrence, "Robotic Solutions on the Farm, *Journal Star*, April 19, 2014, http://www.pjstar.com/article/20140419/NEWS/140418863/-1/business.

Chapter 14 The Problem in the Age of Robots is Us

Brain, Marshall, *Manna: Two Visions of Humanity's Future*, BYG Publishing, Amazon Kindle, 2012. http://www.amazon.com/Manna-Two-Visions-Humanitys-Future-ebook/dp/B007HQH67U.

"Defense spending," SIPRI, The Stockholm International Peace Research Institute: http://www.sipri.org/yearbook/2013/03.

Guaranteed minimum income: See http://en.wikipedia.org/wiki/Guaranteed_minimum_income.

Lovelock, James, *The Vanishing Face of Gaia*, Basic Books, New York, 2009.

Chapter 15 Envirostability

Brynjolfsson, Erik and McAfee Andrew, *The Second Machine Age: Work, Progress, and Prosperity in a Time of Brilliant Technologies*, Norton, New York, 2014.

Carroll, Lewis, *Alice's Adventures in Wonderland and Through the Looking Glass*. Available as one book or two books at low cost from several publishers and free as an ebook because it is out of copyright.

"Carbon is forever," *Nature Reports Climate Change*, http://www.nature.com/climate/2008/0812/full/climate.2008.122.html.

Lovelock, James. He has written several books on Gaia. The latest one, and the one I used in research for this book, is: *The Vanishing Face of Gaia: A Final Warning*, Basic Books, New York, 2009.

Segrè, Gino, *A Matter of Degrees*, Viking, New York, 2002.

Smil, Vaclav, *The Earth's Biosphere*, The MIT Press, Cambridge, Mass., 2002.

Tyrrell, Toby, *On Gaia: A Critical Investigation of the Relationship between Life and Earth*, Princeton University Press, Princeton and Oxford, 2013.

Van Valen, Leigh, "A new evolutionary law," *Evolutionary Theory*, 1,1973. http://leighvanvalen.com/evolutionary-theory/.

Chapter 16 To Go Where No Person has Gone Before

Brumfiel, Geoff, "The Insane and Exciting Future of the Bionic Body," *Smithsonian Magazine,* September, 2013, http://www.smithsonianmag.com/innovation/the-insane-and-exciting-future-of-the-bionic-body-918868/?all.

Callaway, Even, "Telomerase reverses ageing process," *Nature,* November 28, 2010, http://www.nature.com/news/2010/101128/full/news.2010.635.html.

Corbyn, Zoë, "Craig Venter: 'This isn't a fantasy look at the future. We are doing the future,'" *The Observer* (UK), October 12, 2013, http://www.theguardian.com/science/2013/oct/13/craig-ventner-mars.

Dececchi, Alexander and Larsson, Hans C. E., "Body and limb size dissociation at the origin of birds: Uncoupling allometric constraints across a macroevolutionary transition," *Evolution* (international journal of organic evolution), May 28, 2013, http://onlinelibrary.wiley.com/doi/10.1111/evo.12150/abstract.

Grossman, Lev, "2045: The Year Man Becomes Immortal," *Time,* February 10, 2011. http://content.time.com/time/magazine/article/0,9171,2048299,00.html.

Flora, Michael, "Project Orion: Its Life, Death, and Possible Rebirth," http://www.islandone.org/Propulsion/ProjectOrion.html.

Pontin, Jason, "Why We Can't Solve Big Problems," *MIT Technology Review*, October 24, 2012, http://www.technologyreview.com/featuredstory/429690/why-we-cant-solve-big-problems/.

"Project Orion (nuclear propulsion)," *Wikipedia*, http://en.wikipedia.org/wiki/Project_Orion_(nuclear_propulsion).

Venter, J. Craig, *Life at the Speed of Light: From the Double Helix to the Dawn of Digital Life*, Viking, New York, 2013.

Chapter 17 A New Beginning

Diamond, Jared, *Collapse*, Penguin Books, New York, 2006.

Kilham, Larry, *MegaMinds: How to Create and Invent in the Age of Google*, Amazon Kindle, 2010.

Wilson, E.O., "Is Humanity Suicidal?" *New York Times Magazine*, May 30, 1993, pp. 23-29, http://www.mysterium.com/suicidal.html.

ACKNOWLEDGEMENTS

First, special thanks go to Bob Eisenstein, John Schultz and Grant Holland who read the book and made helpful comments. They are scientists and engineers and focused on the technical issues. I also thank Amy Swapp who edited the book and brought her talent for storytelling to bear. I greatly benefitted from the discussions I have had with friends at the Santa Fe Institute including Jeremy Sabloff, Geoffrey West, Jennifer Dunne, and Paul Hooper. Through it all, my wife Betsy has been my rock solid advisor and cheerleader.

ABOUT THE AUTHOR

Larry Kilham founded three companies and is a holder of three patents. Many of those efforts required innovative use of computers, and as early as the 1960s he was researching artificial intelligence. He graduated from the University of Colorado and MIT. He has written five books. Two are about creativity and invention, and three are a series of adventures featuring near-future AI. More information about his books can be found at www.FutureBooks.info.

Larry and his wife Betsy live in Santa Fe, New Mexico. He is a corporate consultant, a member of the American Chemical Society, and is keenly interested in AI, ecology, global resources and the science of complexity.

www.ingramcontent.com/pod-product-compliance
Lightning Source LLC
Chambersburg PA
CBHW021405170526
45164CB00002B/505